TO C(
(

WITH LU...

50 SHADES OF GRADES

My Journey Through Wacademia

Andrew R. Nixon, EdD.

50 Shades of Grades
My Journey Through Wacademia
Andrew R. Nixon, EdD

Cover Photo:
Top row: Lloyd Roberts, Denny Terzich, Tom Campano , Judy Forsythe, Miss Heidrich, Judy Pierosh, Patricia Fodella, Marian Pastore, Ronald Knight.

Middle Row: Larry Triglia, Chester Ignatzek, Larry Grimenstine, Danny Costello, Frank Fiore, Yours Truly Andy Nixon, Dominic Leccia, Dennis Nagy, Paul Bratton, Raymond Guffey Ed Auslander (sent me the photo)

Front row: Richard Baxter, Judy Forsythe?, Louise Socan, Charlotte Laubham, Mary Louise Miller, Andrea Papson, Barbara Cundra, Clyde Desiderio, Billy Alahouzes.

For information on getting permission for reprints and excerpts, contact ARN@50shadesofgrades.com

ISBN: 978-0-9890854-0-3

"I never let schooling interfere with my education"
—Mark Twain

"I could have been a Rhodes Scholar, except for my grades"
—Duffy Daugherty

"I feel that education needs an overhaul – courses are obsolete and grades are on their way out."
—Kent McCord

"What makes a child gifted and talented may not always be good grades in school, but a different way at looking at the world and learning."
—Senator Chuck Grassley

"Not everyone who wanders is lost."
—J. R. R. Tolkein

Foreword

What follows is my story; a boy who was born too soon, who grew too slowly, and who was an alien by virtue of being a right-brain person in a left-brain world as well as a left-hander in a right handed world. The events depicted in this book are as I remember them. My life path, from beginning as a poor student, navigating through the ranks of academia, and finally having achieved the ultimate degree in education, was shaped by a series of accidental occurrences. The story also tells how grades one receives in school do not necessarily predict achievement. Academia can be both out of sync and out of touch with students.

Whether a straight-A student or one whose grades come in fuzzy shades, it is rare that one focuses on exactly where life's journey will take him. For most, life is shaped by happenstance or a series of accidents; who or when to marry, when children come along, professional and personal opportunities, and setbacks. In that sense, my journey through life might not be so different than that of many others.

The story begins two generations earlier in a part of the world that was at various times called Austria, Hungary, The Austro-Hungarian Empire, Yugoslavia, and most recently a group of independent countries established after the breakup of the former Yugoslavia. People of that era were graded on such things as their ability to earn a living, their physical attractiveness, or their level of commitment to a religion. They were also perniciously graded on their circumstance of birth – whether born with a silver spoon in their mouth or a pick and shovel in their hand.

Grades were also a benchmark of whether or not one's work performance was "up to grade." Students were not given grades but were tutored individually. Once their studies were complete they went into the work force with a recommendation from a tutor instead of a transcript.

William Farish, a tutor at Cambridge University in 1792, is given credit for developing the modern grading system. By assigning grades, he would not have to get to know his students as well as other teachers, thereby allowing him to process many more students in a shorter period of time. His clever "invention" caught on in America in the nineteenth century and ballooned in the twentieth.

These days, grades are typically assigned a letter value, A, B, C, D, or F. Some grading systems include percentages that may or may not translate to letter grades. A 70 percent can be equivalent to a "C" grade in one system or a "D" grade in another. Universities frequently assign a number grade point, meaning letter grades can be converted to or from a number value, (A=4.0, B=3.0, C=2.0, D=1.0, F=0.0). Grade points can be on a five-point scale, or a three-point scale.

In the mid-twentieth century a popular grading system was referred to as ESNU; E (Excellent) S (Satisfactory), N or NI (Needs Improvement), or U (Unsatisfactory)

Grades may be weighted or un-weighted, and might include plus (+) or minus (–) after each letter grade, with the exception of F. Grades might also be I (Incomplete), FN (Failure, Non-attendance), X (audit) or W (Withdrawal). Samford University, near Birmingham, Alabama, offers 21 different grades that could be earned by students.

Grades can also come in colors: A "Red 70" can be a passing grade that is on the verge of failure. Red and Blue Ribbon, Gold, Silver, Bronze, and Platinum medals, can be considered colored grades. It is clear that more than Fifty Shades of Grades can be identified in evaluating achievement. What William Farish began has become so scattered in education that it begs for a new name. Dictonary.com defines the word wacky as "odd, irrational, or crazy." My own definition of the grading process in academic education is "Wacademia."

I have had many failures in my life; earning failing grades among them. Indeed, my failures have far outnumbered my successes. However, over the years I have committed myself to the philosophy that failure is the tuition we pay for success, provided we learn from our failures. I have neither cited nor focused on my failures in this book, rather, I've noted some of my successes and the joy they have provided.

INTRODUCTION

As the twentieth century dawned and the excesses of the Gay Nineties of the Nineteenth Century began to fade, high hopes proliferated in many parts of the world. Other areas of the world did not hold such high expectations. The first decade and a half of the new century saw an uneasy peace in the Balkan countries, the culmination of which was the First World War.

An industrial revolution was dawning in the United States. Pittsburgh, Pennsylvania, steel capital of the world, once described by Boston writer James Parton as "Hell with the lid off" was thriving. Despite the putrid air, or perhaps because of it, the burgeoning steel industry needed employees – lots of them. Poor whites from Appalachia, African Americans from the south (which was only a few decades removed from the Emancipation Proclamation of 1863) and farmers from New England were among the many who flocked to the steel mills along the Monongahela, Allegheny, and Ohio rivers, but still more workers were needed. One solution was to recruit in the rural villages of Eastern Europe. Italy, the huge Austro-Hungarian Empire, and other Balto-Slavic countries had struggled economically in the early twentieth century and many strapping young, uneducated men were promised streets paved with gold and given third class passage to America if they would agree to work in the mills. Among the recruits were Peter Vucinovich and Marion Nikolich, my maternal and paternal grandfathers respectively.

Peter Vucinovich, my maternal grandfather, came first, shortly after the turn of the century. He had been his family's first born in the impoverished village of Stabanza, Bosnia, to a Serbian couple. His mother died when he was a small child and his father remarried. At age eight Peter left home and went to work as a stable boy on a horse farm in Germany. He worked there, until his mid-teens then left and bounced around Europe doing odd jobs as a hod-carrier (an entry level job that required heavy boxes of wet cement carried up ladders to masons), laborer and whatever else he could find. Exactly how or when Peter got to America is a little sketchy, but he ended up in Clairton, Pennsylvania working in the local steel mill and living in a boarding house.

In another part of Eastern Europe that would later become Croatia, Marion Nikolich who stood 6'2" and was built like Adonis, married his sweetheart Mara at age 19. He then enlisted in the Austro-Hungarian Army and fulfilled his military obligation as a Medic. By the time the First World

War had ended and steel mill recruiters came to their village of Lovrec' the couple had one son, Marko. Despite the fact that Marion had several years remaining on his Reserve military obligation, he decided to take the offer of the steel company and go to America to start a new life in a land with new opportunities. Once he was established and had saved enough money he would return to Lovrec' to gather his wife and son.

After some time had passed Marion did return to his village to plan a return with his family, but was told by village elders that he was listed as AWOL from the Army and would be arrested the following morning. That night he took the "Midnight Express" and high-tailed it out of Lovrec' to the Italian seaport of Trieste, then boarded a steamer ahead of the Military Police. Soon he was safely back in America. Not long thereafter he sent for his wife and son.

Marion was in charge of the finances in his family so he sent a ticket for his wife Mara and their six-year old son, Marko. Mara's brother escorted Mara and Marko from the village to the seaport of Trieste where they boarded the ship for America, third class (steerage) of course.

Upon arrival in New York Mara and Marko had train tickets that Marion had sent them, which would provide transport to meet him, but they had no cash. Strict immigration rules required several criteria in order to be permitted to disembark the ship. For example, each passenger in steerage was required to pass a physical examination and answer a brief set of questions to prove they were mentally competent and not a convict. A translator asked the questions. The procedure presented no problem for Mara and Mark until they came to the last requirement – everybody who disembarked the ship must have in their possession at least $10.00 in cash. It was meant to prevent vagrancy. However, Mara had no cash, only her train ticket, and was thus detained with her son. It took five days until the shipping company was able to track down Marion and have him wire the money to get his wife and son out of hock! During that time manifest records show that the pair, although kept in detention, was fed three meals per day and housed at the expense of the shipping company.

Meanwhile, my maternal grandfather, Pete, had taken up residence in an ethnic boarding establishment that housed several people who had a common culture and language. The owners, Miko and Bara Brezovich, were from the Croatian village of Sisljavic on the Kupa River near the industrial center of Karlovac. They had been in the United States for a decade and had left the "old country" after the death of their infant son. Their five-year old daughter Kata had stayed behind with her grandmother. The young couple set out to make their fortune in America and Miko soon found work in the coalmines near Clairton, Pennsylvania. One day while digging coal, a large slab of slate became dislodged and fell, hitting Miko in the neck and causing him to be physically incapacitated and unable to continue work as a miner. Of course, there was no insurance or worker compensation in those days, so the couple took their meager savings and opened a boarding house. Housing was so scarce that each of the dozen or so beds in the boarding house, which was little more than an abandoned railroad car, was used twice. When the day shift left for work the night shift slept and vice versa.

By this time the year was 1914 and the cute little five-year old who had been left with Granny was now a 15-year old rebellious teen who had dropped out of school in the second grade and was running the streets with her boyfriend. The parents and grandmother felt it was in the best interest to bring their daughter Kata to America, so they made a deal with their boarder, Pete. If he would pay for the girl's passage, they would bring her to the United States as his bride.

As war was appearing imminent in Europe, Kata's parents arranged for her to come to America. The teen had a precocious nature and lack of fear about her that belied her age. She traveled by rail with a family who was also immigrating, to Le Havre, France. There she boarded the S.S. La Savoie and left Europe, her country, her past, and her boyfriend behind for what she thought was to be a lark. Kata was to become the child bride of 24-year old Peter Vucinovich. She had escaped Eastern Europe, an even more tenuous situation, and arrived in New York City just two days before Archduke Ferdinand was assassinated in Sarajevo. That act would be the catalyst that began the "War to End All Wars."

The marriage arrangement solved several problems for Pete. He was shy and rarely dated. He had saved most of his money while living in the boarding house for the past seven years, as he neither drank nor gambled, and since nearly 100 percent of the single immigrants who came to the United States during that era were men, few opportunities for marriage existed. He agreed to the wedding arrangements.

One "minor" problem remained to be solved. Kata, the rebellious teen had a boyfriend who she saw as her intended. There was no way the recalcitrant teen would leave her boyfriend to marry some "old goat" of 24. Her parents and grandmother agreed to omit that part of the story. They simply said that she would be going to America to visit her parents. Kata agreed.

The deception was realized once she arrived in the boarding house. Kata flat refused to marry Pete. Her mother said, "Daughter, we cannot afford to send you back and there will soon be war in our country so your choices are to marry Pete or sit outside between the railroad tracks and wait for a train to run over you." The teen stomped out of the room and took up a position on the track. As she related this story to me many, many times, she said that she sat and cried for what must have been several hours. Finally when she was all cried out she returned to the house and agreed to the wedding. Pete and Kata were married in late July and thirteen months after the wedding, August 11, 1915, my mother was born. She was named Ruza, after her deceased paternal grandmother.

BOOMTOWN

Clairton was bursting at the seams with all the new employees who were coming to work in the mill. The immigrants of course settled with those whose language and customs they shared; Italians lived near Italians, Slavs near Slavs, African Americans with African Americans, Germans with Germans, Irish with Irish and so forth. Although we did not think of these enclaves as ghettoes, they followed a pattern much like that of nearby communities and major population centers. The trend began in the mid 19th century with the immigration of Germans and Irish and continued with Middle and Eastern Europeans throughout the 1920s. Clairton soon became an ethnic microcosm of industrial centers throughout America with the steel mills paying most of the taxes, and so the town grew.

Prior to the mills being built along the Monongahela River, Clairton was the site of Central Park, a large riverside amusement park where wealthy Pittsburghers and other area people came to dance and enjoy themselves. Once the mills bought up the riverside property and the park was gone, another site was identified to become Clairton Park, which to this day remains one of the finest and most beautiful picnic and outdoor areas in the greater Pittsburgh area.

The community continued to grow as a rich, culturally diverse middle class community. A high school was built and quickly outgrown. A second, much larger high school was built across the street and what had been the original high school became one of several elementary schools in the community. At its peak, Clairton had a population that approached 25,000 and contained four or five movie theaters, a dozen car dealerships, and nearly two-dozen churches of all denominations, a private parochial school, and commerce to accommodate every citizen's need.

The immigrants who settled for the most part spoke little English besides what was required to survive at work, the market, and to acquire life's necessities. The children of those immigrants were to become part of the so-called Greatest Generation. They were born at the onset of the Great Depression and frequently served as translators for their parents. Many were bi-lingual and spoke smatterings of several languages. An example was the local mortician, Tony Beckavac. His was the primary funeral home for Clairton residents who lived on "The Hill" (as opposed to the north part of Clairton: Wilson and Coal Valley). I was fascinated while attending funerals of immigrants who had lived in

Clairton for many years and had befriended people from other cultures. When the funeral was about to begin, Tony would step to the front of the room and give instructions in English, then give the same instructions in Italian, Serbian, Slovenian, or whatever language was needed to accommodate the mourners. It was a sociological phenomenon.

The children of the immigrants in Clairton were, for the most part, very frugal out of necessity. Money was often scarce due to strikes, layoffs, work stoppages, and the ebbs and flows of the nation's need for steel. With the onset of the 1930s came the Great Depression. The Steel industry faltered as clients worldwide pulled back their steel orders. Shopkeepers walked a fine line between cash and credit. Basic necessities for food and clothing existed but without cash to pay for them shopkeepers either carried longtime customers on credit or lost their businesses when their own debt overwhelmed them. Many immigrants had large families and it was not uncommon to have younger children work for local businesses doing menial labor. Goods were often paid in lieu of wages. The children's meager income was sometimes the family's only source of income. Many lost their homes or could not afford to maintain them. Others moved out of their homes and rented more humble abodes while renting out their own homes and hoping that the tenants would be able to pay the rent.

My mother often related stories of life during the Depression. She and her younger brother, Mike, were hired by Frank Grisnik to clean the bakery after business hours.

Their task included cleaning the floor that was caked with a residue of flour, and other ingredients needed for making bread and baked goods. To ease the drudgery the children would strap scrub brushes to their feet and pretend they were skating. Once the residue was loosened they would scrub the floors. They were paid not in cash but in Grade A flour that allowed their mother to bake bread and cook staples that required flour. My mother and her sisters also worked during the Depression cleaning the windows and floors of the Clairton Hotel, located near the corner of St. Clair and Miller Avenues. The large second story windows opened by swinging out and many is the time they feared they would push too hard and fall.

The little that they earned from such jobs was not enough to offset their father Pete's lack of income. Fortunately, the house was paid for as Pete and Kata had built it themselves with the help of friends and neighbors. Unfortunately, taxes on the house were still due and since they were unable to afford the taxes, they rented out their own house and sought cheaper housing, first in the rural part of Jefferson Borough, then further down the river near Aliquippa. My mother and her father would take the train from Aliquippa to Clairton each month to collect the rent but on more than one occasion the tenants were unable to pay the rent and the eviction process was a difficult, time consuming, and expensive one. Not only did they lose the rent that the tenant had not paid, but the cost of eviction created even a greater financial toll on the family. Somehow, however, they made it through the Great Depression and managed to keep their house on Arch Street that overlooked the mill offices.

When the Great Depression finally came to an end in 1941, it was in large part because America had gone to war and the industrial complex needed war products and materials that would be manufactured by Americans. This also gave a huge boost to the steel industry. But it was a mixed blessing, for as the economy began to improve and the jobs began coming back, many of the men who would fill those jobs would be drafted or volunteer for the military service, leaving behind huge numbers of job vacancies.

However, the Greatest Generation included not only sons, but also the daughters of immigrants; women assumed the roles of police officers, steel workers, truck drivers, construction workers, and nearly every other occupation.

Posters appeared of a young lady dressed in work clothes and using tools. She became "Rosie the Riveter," a symbol of workingwomen who had filled the vacancies left by men gone off to war. In fact, my own mother, whose birth name Ruza had been Americanized to Rose, worked in the steel mill during the war doing what had previously been considered a job that only a man could do.

MY ACCIDENTAL LIFE
BEGINS

I was born a second generation American whose grandparents spoke little English and whose parents were bi-lingual. My birth took place in January 1943, the midst of World War-II in Clairton, a steel mill town along the Monongahela River near Pittsburgh. I was the third child and first boy to be born in the family. My early life was unremarkable except for the usual childhood traumas. There was no kindergarten in Clairton in 1948 so I started the first grade at age five, which was way too early for me, as I was a late bloomer. Because of the premature beginning I never did well in school. Teachers did their best not to label children as remedial, but we all knew that the Bluebird reading group was the lowest.

My grades did not improve much as I progressed through junior high and high school, and the gap between my academic prowess and that of my classmates became wider.

I was what my high school counselor called, "not college material." My grades suggested I might be better suited as a forest ranger, a ditch digger, or perhaps a shepherd, but not a college student.

None of that meant anything to my father who had dropped out of school in the eighth grade and insisted his son would attend college. I figured I would dodge the college scene by announcing plans to join the Marine Corps. It did not work. My father squelched that idea and began to browbeat me to plan for college. That was one of the many areas of contention between my father and myself. I agreed with the counselor who told me I was not college material and my grades supported her assessment. But my father would have none of it. He did not accept the generally accepted rules of society. His philosophy was to get to a place by hook or by crook ("Damn the protocol, full speed ahead!") and do well once you got there. His argument was that the sons of wealthy and powerful men were placed in positions of authority, although they were often poorly prepared, and they did just fine. So why should his son not be provided the same benefit? I'm certain he would have held our former president, (George W. Bush was never a scholar but was the son of a president) up as an example of his belief.

My father and I had an interesting relationship. He had the misfortune of having his one and only son born with a personality, skills, and abilities exactly the opposite of his own. He had tremendous manual dexterity and could build or create nearly anything. What he could not create, he was able to envision and explain to craftsmen who could create it. I on the other hand was the exemplar of poor coordination, so much so that if I were to eat an ice cream cone, surely it would hit my forehead instead of my mouth. He was single minded and focused; I was scattered. He saw the world in black and white; I saw the world in shades of grey and in multiple shades of color.

Still, we had some good times during my preteen years. My father was a great storyteller. He told of his experience on the police force when a fellow officer, an immigrant whose English language skills were limited and whose writing ability was practically nil. The cop, named Tony Katich, was sent in his squad car to Mendelsohn Avenue to investigate an injured animal. When he arrived he discovered that a horse had been struck and killed by a delivery truck. Tony did the investigation and then came the dreaded part of his job – writing a report of the incident. Tony's reports were brief and he began to write, "Hors kilt Mndls…" He scratched out the street name and tried, without success to for a spelling close enough to be recognized as "Mendelsohn." Finally, in frustration he took a rope from the trunk of his squad car, tied one end around the dead animal's neck and the other around the bumper of his police car and dragged the carcass two blocks to North Fourth Street. He then completed his report, "Hors kilt 4 St."

Because my father was a Special Equipment Operator for the Street Department of the City of Clairton he had access to the garage in which the vehicles were kept during his "off hours." He began a Saturday ritual, first with my older sisters then with me. At age twelve or thirteen he would take one of us with him to the garage where City vehicles were stored. He would open the huge garage door and carefully back out the grader, the high lift, and perhaps a dump truck, then pull his car into the garage and wash it with the help of the child who accompanied him. After the car was cleaned and the equipment returned, our reward would be to drive the car home. The distance from the City garage to home was less than a mile but to a twelve or thirteen year old behind the wheel it seemed like quite a long ride.

As a family we occasionally drove to Battle Creek and Flint, Michigan where we had relatives. On those trips my father would sometimes let one of the underage siblings drive part of the way. One trip, as we sped along the Ohio Turnpike, my sister Kathy, the second eldest, was given the privilege to drive on the "super-highway." She was in her glory, tooling down the high way at 65 miles per hour as she moved into the left lane and passed a couple of semi tractor-trailers. My father told her to flip the turn signal and return to the right lane and she began to do so – without first checking the mirror. The screeching of tires and an angry blast from the truck's air horn led my father to grab the steering wheel, as she had cut off the truck nearly driving it into a ditch. Sometimes the best laid plans of mice and men often go awry.

My father lived his single-minded philosophy. White is white and black is black and there are no shades of gray.

During the Great Depression he felt that his inability to find work was due to his ethnic last name so he went to visit a relative in Detroit in hopes of finding work there. Each day he'd show up at a plant in nearby River Rouge and watch while the few men who were called for a job all seemed to have Anglo-sounding names. Of course it did not occur to him that 80 percent of the men at the show-up who had Anglo-sounding names did not get called either. This experience nevertheless cemented his belief that only men with Anglo names were hired. He noted the name of the foreman who did the hiring (also with an Anglo-sounding name), looked the name up in the local phone book, and determined where the foreman lived.

About 30 minutes before the foreman was to return home from work, my father, then a handsome, strapping lad of 19, knocked on the door and asked if Mr. so-and-so was home. The wife said he was due shortly and my father, turning on the charm, apologized for the intrusion but said he was new in town and had hoped her husband might be able to direct him to some sort of job. The wife invited him to wait on the screened-in porch and brought out a pitcher of fresh lemonade.

By the time the husband arrived, the 19-year-old lad had the wife totally smitten. She said, "Honey, Mr. Nixon (He had Anglicized "Nikolich," which in the Slavic languages literally means son of Nick, to "Nixon") here, has traveled all the way from Clairton, Pennsylvania in search for work. I'm sure you could find him SOMETHING to do in the plant, couldn't you?"

The foreman thought he'd quickly dismiss the brash youngster and said, "The only opening we have right now is for a crane-man. Have you ever operated an overhead crane?"

"Oh yes, Sir," he lied through his teeth, "My uncle runs a crane in a mill in Pittsburgh and he showed me how to operate it."

The foreman was trapped by this slick youngster but went on to explain (just in case the kid really was a hot-shot crane operator), "Well I don't care what kind of experience you've had in the past, our policy here at National Tube is that as a new hire you'll be on probation and operate a crane under the supervision of a senior crane operator for 30 days, then take a test that you must pass to continue. Be at the gate at 8:00 a.m. tomorrow morning and your name will be one of four called." And so at age 19, having never seen an overhead crane, let alone operated one, "Andy Nixon" was hired as a crane operator.

The next morning my father showed up at the gate and his new name "Nixon" was one of the four Anglo names called. The rest of the 200 or so men left to return the following day in hopes that they might win the job lottery in days to come.

Once inside the mill the young man was directed to the crane where his supervising crane operator worked. As he climbed the ladder into the cab of the crane he had a nervous smile. Once atop the crane the men shook hands and from under his coat my father pulled a fifth of the finest whiskey he was able afford. He handed it to the senior crane operator and spoke first, "I have not run a crane before but I'm a quick study. Please don't give me away. All I ask is that you teach me what you can and, in 30 days, give me a fair shot. If I can't do it I'll disappear."

The senior operator, a middle-aged man who liked his whiskey, paused, smiled, and said, "Kid, you have balls! I'll teach you what I can." Thirty days later my father made the grade and became a 19-year old certified crane operator. He worked throughout the rest of the Great Depression at National Tube in Ecorse, Michigan, a mill that was busy filling government contracts.

After several years as a crane operator my father had bought a new car, sent money home to his family, and lived the life of a bachelor with money in his pockets. When work began to pick up in Clairton he returned home as the Great Depression was drawing to a close. He bluffed his way into a job with the Police Department and served on the home front in that capacity during World War II. He held that position until the regular officers returned from the war and claimed their old jobs. My father tried to stay with the police department but was instead transferred to the Street Department as a Special Equipment Operator, a job that he held for more than 40 years.

THE ACCIDENTAL COLLEGE STUDENT

My father started grooming me to plan to become a college student from the time I was in the ninth grade, when the firstborn in the family entered Millersville State Teachers College. His philosophy that anybody could attend college or, as he had done, have a successful career, might have made the grade for him as well as for children of the rich and powerful. I did not believe it would work for me so I did everything possible to sabotage his plan for my college education. I resisted or simply did not respond each time he brought up the topic. By my junior year in high school I began to lobby to go to the Marines after high school. Whenever I would bring the subject of military service up his response was, "That is for rum-heads. You don't see the sons of Senators in the service. They all go to college and let the poor ethnic kids go to war." Still, I simply could not picture myself in a college classroom.

One day during my senior year in high school I asked my classmate, Betsy Norris, about her post-high school plans and she responded that she would be attending a church-affiliated university in Utah. She said that although the university was 2,000 miles away she looked forward to attending and her parents were excited about it as well. A light bulb lit up in my mind. A school sponsored by a religion not my own, located 2,000 miles from home! She continued, "You know I'm a Mormon, right?"

I looked aghast and said, "YOU'RE A MORMON???? Then why do you wear makeup and not dress in black?" (I had seen the so-called "Plain people" in Eastern, Pennsylvania where my sisters attended college).

Betsy laughed, "You're so silly. I'm a Mormon, not a Mennonite."

I quickly responded, "I knew that. I was just teasing, (although didn't, and I hadn't been)." Then added, "Where is this school again?

She said, "Provo, Utah."

"Uh, Utah!" I answered, "Isn't that out past Chicago somewhere?"

She laughed again, "Yes, in fact it is 2,000 miles from Clairton. The school is Brigham Young University."

This could be the very reason I was looking for to get my father off my back. Surely he would not permit me to go to such a university. My father never was much on organized religion. He blamed the Catholic religion for most of his family's ills, disliked priests in general and became a

Presbyterian in large part because that is where the movers and shakers of the town attended church.

I began working out a plan; making my first trip to the school library and asking the librarian about this university, sending for information, poring over articles about BYU, and designing a fail-safe plan that would make my choice of this particular university so repugnant to my father that he would refuse and I would join the Marine Corps. I would blackmail my father by saying the only way I would attend college would be at this school. No way would he agree!

Finally my plan was ready. I sat down with my father one evening and presented him with my own ultimatum. I would apply to college but it would have to be the one I selected. He agreed and I moved in for the kill as I said, "Brigham Young University in Provo, Utah. It is 2,000 miles away and run by the Mormon Church." Unbeknownst to me, he had learned of my sudden interest in BYU and had done some checking of his own.

He responded, "Ok."

I was stunned and wanted to say, "Is that your final answer?" But although I was down I was not out. I had not anticipated his agreement with my choice but I had another part of my plan yet to be implemented. BYU was an excellent school and quite frankly, my grades were so poor that there was no way that I would be admitted, and if by some fluke I were to be admitted I would surely flunk out after the first term and be far from the grasp of my hometown, where I had never been successful, and away from the influence of my father.

Although my father only had eight years of formal education, he had other skills; he was both crafty and manipulative of any system. Once he had gotten wind of my interest in BYU he began a campaign of his own, asking local Mormon leaders and educators to write letters on my behalf designed to compensate for my poor grades. He even asked the counselor for a letter; the one who repeated to him what she had told me, that I was not "college material." My father went on about how denying a person an opportunity was something an educator should not do and she finally relented and agreed to write a letter that "would not hurt him." I was accepted for admission. I could not believe it!

I was not above shucking and jiving for a grade or playing the system. When I was in the eighth or ninth grade I took a required Government class from Lou Balta. Report cards were about to come out and he called each student up to his desk to tell them how many points they'd accrued and what grade to anticipate. My point total indicated a 65, which was a failing mark. I asked him if I could "borrow" ten points against my next grading period's score. That would give me a 75 (low C) and I would make up the difference the following marking period. Mr. Balta was so impressed with my ingenuity that he "gave" me the extra points.

I do not believe that the letters alone would have overcome my poor high school transcript. Rather, I have another theory about what might have happened. Clairton High School in the 1950s did not give letter grades but percentages. The transcript had a conversion table noted that 95-100=A, 85-

94=B, 75-84=C, 70-74=D and below 70 percent was Failure. But the conversion table was written in small print and my theory is that whoever converted my high school transcript grades to the more widely accepted A, B, C, D, F, ignored the conversion table and simply used the standard 90-100=A, 80-90=B, etc. Thus all my 70 grades would have translated as C grades rather than D grades and my high school grade point average would have gotten a considerable boost. But even with the boost I was admitted on academic probation.

So it was that my father insisted that despite my poor grades, despite my counselor telling me I was not college material, despite my extreme dislike for school, and despite the fact that colleges looked for applicants with resumes that were the opposite of my own, I would attend college.

Given the above background, my memoirs begin the summer of 1960. I had just graduated high school and spent the summer working to save money for college—a place I felt I did not belong but was willing to try.

OFF TO COLLEGE

Once I realized I had actually been admitted to college I began my first self-assessment. I was not happy with my life in Clairton. I was not an athlete. I had few close friends. My relationship with my father was strained. I didn't seem to do anything right or constructive. I didn't want to work in the steel mills and I didn't see a future as a box boy at Haines Super Market nor with an evening job delivering newspapers to paperboys. My options in Clairton were clearly limited. Of course, joining the Marines was my first choice, but going to college would please my father and I would be 2,000 miles away—far enough that nobody in Utah except my classmate Betsy would know my family or me. I could start anew – become whoever I wanted to be. Provo, Utah was looking more and more like my salvation.

Of course there is more than one side to every assessment. So I pondered.... What could the down side be to my leaving home? I was certain that once I left I would never return. Oh, I would come back to visit, but not to live. So what would I be giving up? I loved my mother and was very close to her. It would be difficult to leave her. My maternal grandparents (Little Baba, who was big, and Little Diedo, who was little) were also very special to me. Baba often tended me while my mother worked and Diedo always made me feel like I was the apple of his eye. Ok, what else? My best buddy Jay? He was going into the Army. Gerry Grunsky? He wasn't really a close friend. He had promised to go to BYU with me then backed out. The rumor was that he had not been accepted because of his Catholic faith, which was of course not true. I was really upset with Gerry and felt like he'd let me down. At least had he gone I would have had a buddy with whom to share the mystery of the unknown. What about..... There was nothing else on the debit side of the ledger.

What about fear of the unknown? It had never crossed my mind. Mystery perhaps, but not fear. Perhaps the Gypsy in me was taking over. To this day I have never feared the unknown concerning different places or cultures, meeting new people and seeing new places. The thought of doing those things lit a fire inside me and I was convinced I was headed for Utah for.... well I didn't know exactly what, but I was willing to give it a try!

CROSSING COUNTRY IN A COVERED RAMBLER WAGON

My parents decided to drive me to Utah for my initial campus introduction, orientation, and registration. They had a new 1960 Rambler station wagon that was sometimes used to deliver papers in addition to the Jeep. That new Rambler was to be the chariot to take us across some seven states, over the Rockies and into the state of Utah.

The Daily News was a daily newspaper published in McKeesport. Each day, six days per week (The Daily News did not publish a Sunday edition) a truck delivered some two thousand papers wrapped in bundles of fifty to our garage. The papers were then counted and a handful of paperboys whose routes were close to our house took their papers and delivered them. The remainder of the papers were counted, repackaged and labeled with the names of the paperboys throughout the city. A stack of loose papers for various stores sat next to the driver. In those days nearly every pharmacy, confectionary, and other type of shop sold daily papers inside the establishments. There were no newspaper vending machines. It took two loads each day to deliver the papers to all the stores and paperboys. On my last day driving the paper route before heading to Utah, the new Rambler station wagon was pressed into service. Somebody drove the Jeep (usually my job) for the first load and I drove the Rambler for the second load. This allowed us to finish early and prepare to leave for Utah early the following morning.

Normally I would drive both loads with a helper who would toss out the bundles of papers at each paperboy's house and would also run papers into the stores while I waited at a stoplight, or double parked if the light turned green. After both runs were completed I would go to Haines Super Market on Route 51 and work as a box-boy until 9 or 10:00p.m.

The day before we left for Utah we were ahead of schedule with the second load. As I drove from store to store, I double-parked while my runner, Roy Potts, took the papers into the shops. Webb's Drug Store, on the corner of State Street and Shaw Avenue was the next to the last stop on the run. The light at the intersection was red so Roy jumped from the car and, as the light changed, I turned the corner and pulled as close to the curb as possible so as not to obstruct traffic. The curb was unusually high—a fact I had not noticed, and as I got close the rocker panel below the door had an unexpected meeting with the curb, pushing the panel below the fender back and preventing the door from opening.

There was Hell to pay when I returned home. My father was absolutely certain that I had damaged the car on purpose so I wouldn't have to go to college. My father never struck me but did his punishment verbally. He let loose in his loud voice with his usual litany of foul and vulgar Anglo Saxon verbiage. I wailed that it had been an accident that could have happened to anybody. Fortunately neighbor Smokey DeCarlo was the proprietor of a body shop that boasted a sign, "See us at your earliest inconvenience." My father took the car to Smokey's Auto Repair for some quick and temporary bodywork. The car was repaired well enough to allow the door to open and close and travel across the country.

At 6:00 a.m. the next morning the Rambler wagon was loaded to the gills, including suitcases on the top luggage rack. We were on our way out of town and the state. I never looked back. Ohio, Indiana, Illinois, Iowa. As a right of passage my father turned the steering wheel over to me and I drove much of the way. I loved every minute. It was the longest stretch of peace I could ever remember having with my father since adolescence. Nebraska, Colorado. The drive across the Rockies was amazing! Steamboat Springs, Hot Sulfur Springs, Denver, and our last night on the road was spent in Craig, Colorado where the following morning we had a breakfast of "Silver Dollar" pancakes (or flapjacks) like I had never had before and the waitress answered most questions with, "You, bet!" an expression I had only heard on television.

Finally we pulled into Provo and found my dorm, Stover

Hall. The Dorm Mother, "Sister" Jean May, was a sweet grandmotherly woman with whom my parents immediately fell in love. They made her promise she would keep an eye on their "Sonny" and keep them informed whenever needs arose. We said our goodbyes and I can still see them driving down the street next to the dorms and turning right onto Highway U.S. 89 that headed up Provo Canyon and eventually connected with highways that took them back home. What I didn't see was something my mother shared with me years later when I had my own family. As soon as they were out of sight my father had to pull the car to the side of the road because he became so emotional, crying and sobbing uncontrollably, that he was unable drive the car. He was never able to express affection to me, but his feelings flowed in the privacy of the car with just his wife to comfort him. They sat and cried for nearly an hour before they composed themselves and drove on, leaving their only son behind at the gates of his manhood.

STRANGER IN A STRANGE LAND

The fall of 1960 was the beginning of my long and arduous trek into manhood. Just as I had been dragged kicking and screaming into the world 17 years earlier, as I really was not ready to be born, so was I anxious about this new world I was about to enter. Prior to discovering that my classmate Betsy Norris was a Mormon the only thing I had known about this group of people was from a movie I had seen on television, "Brigham Young." I seem to remember that most of the men wore beards and the women looked plain, they all rode wagons or pulled carts and called one another "brother" or "sister." I was not sure how much had changed from what had been depicted in the movie as having taken place in 1847.

I would reluctantly start college about the time of the presidential elections. It was Kennedy vs. Nixon, the brash, young, handsome son of a Catholic kingmaker, vs. the serious, stern, sweating Communist-chaser who was clearly representative of the establishment. It would be quite an election but my concerns were much more micro than macro. I was about to begin college in a strange setting, at a university whose religion was foreign to me, and whose culture was so different than what I had grown up in that I sometimes felt like I was on a movie set.

Provo, Utah. A new beginning to be sure, but the culture of Provo in 1960, and of Brigham Young University, was vastly different than that of greater Pittsburgh. Certainly the religious mix was different—that was to be expected. Clairton, Pennsylvania consisted of an environment that was probably 30 percent Catholic, 20 percent Protestant, and the balance a mixture of Jewish, Serbian, Greek, and Russian Orthodox, assorted African American churches, a sprinkling of Baptist and a few agnostic, atheist, and quite a few "couldn't care less." The ethnicity of the Pittsburgh area was a rich mixture of working class Eastern Europeans, Italians, Irish, African Americans and Anglos. Jewish families and ethnic immigrants owned businesses, and Anglos generally held the white-collar jobs. Most children of 1950's Clairton were children or grandchildren of immigrants. Surnames frequently ended with a vowel or with ich or began with O' or Mc. The steel mill was the economic lifeblood of the community and the price of the region's economic prosperity was dirty air. Whenever a house was re-shingled, after the passing of a few months, all shingles on the rooftops would be black regardless of their original color, fresh fallen snow often was gray, and the pungent odor of quencher (quench hardening is a mechanical process in which steel and cast iron alloys are strengthened and hardened. Metals are heated in a blast furnace then sprayed with water to cool. The water bounces into the air and comes to rest as a polluted substance called quencher) filled the air and left a thick residue on car windshields, so much so that when driving through quencher it would become necessary to use the windshield washers and wipers or pull to the side of the road and clean the windshield.

BYU and Provo on the other hand was comprised of nearly 90 percent Mormons (Latter Day Saints) and ethnically mostly English and Scandinavian. Grandparents all spoke unaccented English. Most families had lived in Utah for nearly 100 years. Rooftops retained their original color for decades, and the air was pristine. Culturally the mood was one of conservatism. Pre-marital sex was a no-no, and early marriage with lots of kids was encouraged. I used to describe Provo as a place where "... the air was clean and sex was dirty." The entire population of Provo in 1960 was fewer than 40,000 and BYU students, faculty, and staff represented about 25 percent of that number. Orem was a separate village north of Provo and the highway to Salt Lake City, U.S. 91, was a narrow two-lane winding road that passed through several bucolic villages to the "Point of the Mountain," (the location of Utah State Prison), and beyond. No freeway between Provo and Salt Lake City then existed. Today, from a point south of Provo, north beyond Salt Lake City to Ogden and perhaps even to Brigham City, there lies one big megalopolis on either side of Interstate 15. Population growth has attacked Utah just as it has more urban areas of more populated states. In fact, when I first arrived in Utah in 1960, the entire populations of Utah, Idaho, Wyoming, and Montana combined totaled fewer than two million, or less than that of the city of Philadelphia!

The once pristine air in the Provo valley today receives poor grades from the Environmental Protection Agency, is often stagnant and polluted for weeks due to inversions of the putrid air from car tailpipe emissions and other environmental concerns.

THE ACCIDENTAL
FRESHMAN

My development as a youngster was slow physically, emotionally and developmentally. My best estimate is that I was developmentally three years behind my chronological age in those areas. To boot, I had started the first grade at about 5 ½ years of age and might have been the youngest in my class. Hence, I came to college having lived 17 years but with the sophistication and emotional maturation of a 14-year old. I was 5'11" tall and weighed 128 lbs. soaking wet. My high school academic experience had been considerably less than stellar. Despite the help of the erroneous grade conversion that provided an artificial increase to my grade point average and the boost the myriad of letters my father's campaign had brought, I was still admitted into BYU only as a special student and on academic probation. If I did not maintain a C average or better in my first semester I would be academically dismissed from the university —a fate I fully anticipated. My course load was part time (11 credits) and included a two-hour non-credit course that was designed to teach me study skills and time management. I'm sure I must have learned something from that course but it did not serve as the basis to turn me from non-scholar to scholar. That task was to fall to two quirks of fate.

First, was my accidental discovery that learning is NOT a one-size-fits-all experience. I had barely graduated from Clairton High School and was ill prepared for the rigors of college or college life in or outside academics. My first meeting with an academic advisor was on the day of my first college course registration. He was a pasty-face 22-year-old recently returned missionary who looked deadly serious. He told me that before I could proceed any further I must select a major field of study. In order to select a major I was handed a college catalog and told to select anything "in heavy bold print." I looked down the list of majors published in heavy bold print: Bacteriology (no), Biology (no), Botany (no), Business (no) English (no), and so on down the alphabet until I came to Psychology. I was unsure exactly what Psychology was but I knew (or at least thought I knew) I would be unable to compete in those other majors because of all the brainy kids from high school who were attending college and had done well in those classes. Psychology, however, was something nobody had taken in high school so at least we were on an even footing. That was my logic for selecting my major field of study.

My choice to major in Psychology proved to be fortuitous, as I took a non-credit class in the Psychology of Learning during my freshman year. In that class I learned about left-brain versus right-brain learning and discovered that because I learned that as a right-brain learner I processed information primarily through my ears rather than my eyes. That is, I remember things that I hear much longer and clearer than information that I read. To this day I remember clearly jokes and anecdotes that I heard 50 or 60 years ago but barely remember the plot of a novel I finished a few months ago.

Most of the population, however, is comprised of left-brain learners who learn by reading and processing words into ideas. Thus, left-brain learners developed our system of education for left-brain learners. Hence, in high school and to a large degree undergraduate college work, the primary method of processing information was to read from a book and regurgitate the information that had been read. Since that was not my mode of learning I did poorly under that system. Further, I was just a fair reader at best. But in college, particularly in upper division courses, where the main delivery method (then at least) was lecture, I began to blossom. If a professor took his exams directly from lectures I would get an A in the class. If he took them from the text (as I rarely cracked a textbook throughout college), I would earn a D or an F. I repeated classes I had failed after sitting through various professor's classes to determine the teaching style and seeing how they tested. Then I would retake a failed class from a different professor; one who lectured and took his tests from the lecture. The process was a bit arduous but it did allow me to better tailor the traditional system of education to my method of learning.

As a bonus, the Psychology Department at Brigham Young University was an excellent one, with many young professors who lectured with vigor and published profusely. I took advantage in two ways. First, the department-wide philosophy was to accept neither paper nor assignment that was deemed to be not "publishable." If a student's work did not meet standards it was not graded but edited and returned with suggestions for improvement to make it closer to pub-lishable manuscript quality. A rewrite and resubmission was required as often as needed. Professors were very patient in helping me and from that experience I seemed to be inclined to meeting their writing standards as my required rewrites became fewer and fewer. To further develop my professional writing skills, I volunteered to help professors who were do-ing experimental research, and closely observed their writing styles. The end result was that I learned to write in a profes-sional style and learned more about writing professionally in my undergraduate Psychology major experience than in any other setting including my own Doctoral program.

In high school I had been one of those kids whose every indicator suggested academic failure. In college I discovered that I am a right-brain learner (and left handed to boot) in a left-brain, right-handed world, trying to function in an ed-ucation system designed by left-brain learners for left-brain learners. Even after I caught on how to "play the system" the overall academic experience was not an easy one for me but I persevered.

The second quirk of fate that helped me achieve success in college was the fact that I registered for classes late. Since my high school counselor had decided I was "not college material," I was never taught even the basic survival skills for college. I completed the registration process by first meeting with an academic advisor (the one who told me I needed a major that was selected from those listed "in heavy black print.") The advisor helped me select my courses for that first semester and I listed them on a master card. The next step was one I apparently missed as I went directly to the registrar to pay my tuition and fees. The line for the registrar was long and when I finally arrived at the cashier window she looked through my packet and asked, "Where are your class cards?"

"Class Cards?" I asked blankly. She then patiently explained that all those other long lines that I had bypassed were for departments that handed out a computer card for each class. I had spent a lot of time standing in the registrar's line, so by the time I got to the class card lines most of the classes were filled and closed. The result was that I got what was left, meaning my classes (each one being 50 minutes long) were held at 7:00 a.m., 9:00 a.m., 11:00 a.m., and 3:00 p.m. on Monday, Wednesday, and Friday, and lab classes, including Air Force Reserve Officers Training Corps Leadership Training Tuesday and Thursday afternoon. The registration ordeal had taken me from 8:30 the morning of the last day of registration until 6:00 p.m. that evening.

I was exhausted and when I left the Fieldhouse where the process had taken place. I sat down on the outside steps and wondered if my high school counselor had been correct – perhaps I simply was not college material because this day had been so overwhelming that I don't think I could have survived many more like it.

The good news that was part of the second quirk of fate was that my first Freshman English teacher was an elderly New Zealand expatriate whose class I had selected purely by chance, and because all those taught by full tenured professors had been closed. Her class was one of the "overload" classes that had been added at the last moment. Mrs. McKay (whom was addressed as "Sister" as the entire faculty were addressed either as Doctor or Sister or Brother followed by their last names) was kindly, encouraging, and took a special interest in me. During the semester she told me that my writing assignments of required weekly themes were exceptional and she further told me that I had a talent for writing.

I was stunned. No teacher, save Mrs. Bayless, my high school English and Drama teacher, had ever encouraged me to do anything academic. Mrs. McKay even had one of my themes published in the school paper. I worked beyond my limitations in her class and earned an "A." At the same time I was writing and rewriting assignments for my Psychology classes and further developing my writing skills. Upon completing my first semester at BYU I had earned better than a 3.0 (B) average, the best grades I had ever gotten! I was removed from academic probation and began the spring semester as a regular student.

The spring semester began with registration again. This time I was prepared with a course list and knew the registration drill. I attempted to register for Mrs. McKay's English 102 class to get more of the same treatment that I had enjoyed during first term, but since she was neither the holder of a doctorate nor a regular tenured professor of the English Department, she was given classes only after all the regular professors' classes had been filled. This called for some creative strategy. Right-brain people are typically creative.

I decided that since I was not as academically astute as my fellow students, I would have to be more street-wise and figure a way to enroll in her class surreptitiously. I discovered that one could drop and add classes within the first five days of the semester with no fees or penalties, but to add additional classes beyond that period cost an additional late fee. So I registered for any English 102 class but did not attend. Rather, I stayed in contact with Mrs. McKay and once she was given her overload class assignment, I simply dropped the English 102 class in which I had enrolled in and replaced it with Mrs. McKay's class. Got my class. No fees or penalties. System beaten.

My self-confidence was at an all time high. Remember the Sinatra song, "That's Life?" Parts of the lyrics include, "I've been a puppet, a pirate, a pauper, a poet, a pawn and a king...."Well, at this particular moment I was a king.

Because of the fact that my other class grades that year

were good and I had ended my freshman year with the best grades I had ever received, I wanted more college, as much as I could get and as soon as I could get it. Brigham Young University had given me something I had never had before —a good report card! And I was doing it by competing with the academically elite from around the country and around the word. It never ceases to amaze me that my despite my mediocre grades in Clairton High School I had absorbed enough knowledge to compete successfully with the brains (the word "nerd" had not yet been invented) in college.

I begged my parents to allow me to stay in Provo for summer school to make up for credits missed due to my part time status when I first enrolled on academic probation. I told them I would find a job to help defray expenses and they agreed. That summer I took a few psychology classes, and entered my second year as a full-fledged fulltime college sophomore in good academic standing. I received straight "A" grades in Psychology classes during the summer. My Psych 101 class had earned me a "C" grade the previous semester (the prof took his exams mostly from the text as well as lectures) but during the summer I had taken several upper division Psychology courses (all exams taken from the lectures with the text as a supplement) and actually enjoyed school for the first (and possibly only) time in my life. As I soon realized, upper division courses require research and writing. I was still not much more than an average reader but my writing skills had improved dramatically due to Mrs. McKay's tutoring and the Psychology Department's rewrite philosophy, and my vocabulary had grown as well.

My freshman year was clearly one of transition. When one changes incrementally it is often difficult to note the changes as they occur. I flew home that first Christmas and was surprised at how everything in Clairton appeared to have changed—yet stayed the same. My parents gave me a surprise 18th birthday party a month early but my friends were mostly gone to the military or college. I knew from that moment I would never return to Clairton to live, as it was I who had changed, not Clairton.

COLLEGE LIFE—
MORE THAN CLASSES

Upon my arrival to the Brigham Young University campus I was assigned to a dorm, the name of which was Stover Hall. BYU was in a period of rapid growth. The student population had doubled to 11,000 students in the previous decade or so. More dorm space was needed so a complex of half a dozen or so dorms, named Helaman Halls, had been built in spoke-like fashion with a student services center, Cannon Center, in the middle. The buildings had just been built the year before my arrival so everything was fresh, new, and every room had a telephone that could receive long-distance calls but only make them if the charges were reversed.

My dorm roommate had been pre-selected at random. Wayne Shepard was a freshman from North Sacramento, California, and a guard on the basketball team. His brother,

Wayland, was a scholarship athlete on the football team and, as is common at BYU, had played football a year or two, gone on a mission, then returned to BYU to complete his education and play the remainder of his eligibility. Like many other BYU athletes in his situation Wayland had married and had a child. A large percentage of BYU athletes follow that scenario. According to National Collegiate Athletic Association (NCAA) rules a college athlete has five calendar years to complete four years of eligibility. Once an athlete either practices with a team or enrolls at a university, the five-year "clock" begins to tick. With very few exceptions, the clock may not stop for any reason. There are some situations for which an athlete may appeal to have a year reinstated but such appeals are rarely granted. The only things that can routinely stop the athlete's eligibility clock are active military service or a church mission. It is not uncommon for over half of the athletes on the BYU athletic teams to be returned missionaries, married, and two years older and more mature than the typical college athlete. Some sports writers and pundits have criticized the NCAA for allowing the church mission exemption to eligibility rules as BYU is the only school that uses it, but the NCAA has stood fast and the policy remains in place.

My designated roommate Wayne was from North Sacramento where he played sports with another Latter Day Saint scholarship athlete, Jim Kimmel. Jim was a football player and both he and Wayne were placed in the same dorm on the same floor, and in the same wing. Wayne was to have roomed with me and Jim was assigned another freshman from Sacramento, Phil Ruiz. But before Wayne and I had met, they convinced Phil that it would make more sense for the two athletes to room together and Phil room with the "new kid from Pittsburgh" (me). Phil Ruiz thereby became my roommate. He was 6'2" and easily weighed 200 lbs. At 5'11" and 128 pounds soaking wet I was a mere wisp of a kid. Phil's heritage was Hispanic but his family had been in California long before mine had come to America from Eastern Europe. He was staunch in his religious beliefs; I was not. In short we did not share much in common.

We were the Odd Couple before the Paul Simon play had ever been written. Phil was meticulous about his housekeeping, his clothing, personal hygiene, courses, schedules, etc. He was highly organized and rigid. He even ironed his socks! I on the other hand was a laid back slob. My mother and sisters had always done household chores for me. My only chore was to empty the garbage after dinner and I learned that if I went to the bathroom after dinner and waited long enough somebody would do that chore on my behalf.

At age 17 I had never washed a sock, ironed a shirt, or cooked a meal. My personal hygiene was lacking and I rarely cleaned my half of the dorm room. It must have been pure Hell for poor Phil who even washed and ironed his underwear and had a spotless, well-organized half of a dorm room. His attitude toward me went from parental to pathetic to hostile. After a particularly slovenly episode on my part he finally became so irate that he taped a line down the center of the room and told me I was never to cross to his side! What a burden I must have been for Phil. To exacerbate matters, as a prank I hid a container of milk inside his closet and the stench became overwhelming. He never did locate the source of the stench and when he could no longer stand it (he thought a rodent had somehow wedged itself inside a wall and died), he had the dorm mother call maintenance to tear out the wall if necessary. I quietly removed the rancid milk carton and tossed it down the trash chute. The maintenance crew was baffled as to the source of the odor and by the time they had arrived it had mostly dissipated. Phil might have had a suspicion that I was the cause of it but he never voiced that opinion to me. By that time we probably were not speaking to one another and he was anxiously waiting for the school year to end so he could move off campus and find a new roommate.

MY FUTURE BEST FRIEND
SANDY

Our next-door neighbors in the dorm were Lonnie Carter; an African American from Houston and a 6' 2" ethnic Chinese lad, who had been born in Shanghai and reared in Lima, Peru after his family fled the Chinese communist government. Sandy was also young and immature as a freshman. At 17 he and I were the youngest freshmen in the dorm, except for Marlow Ashton, a 16 year-old genius from Canada. Sandy and I were both flakes, both slobs, and both clearly not a part of the Mormon establishment. We became fast friends and have stayed so to this day. Sandy was also as bright as he was irresponsible. He would sign up for a full load of classes and not attend, thereby earning an "F" average and be placed on academic probation. The following semester he would repeat the classes and earn an "A" in each thereby removing himself from probation. He was the most amazing academic specimen I've ever known. Sandy left BYU with a Bachelor of Science degree in Political Science and, like me, a marginal grade point average. With political connections from influential friends of his family he was admitted to a graduate program at the University of Utah and took that time to buckle down, study well, and complete a Master's degree in Communications. He pursued the field of Advertising, starting with what was then the largest Ad agency in the world—Young and Rubicam in New York. Sandy opened offices for them and worked in Rio, Paris, Brussels, Milan, and Montreal. He was doing his second tour in Brussels when he wrote and told me he was expecting a move soon and anticipated returning to America. When I next heard from him, he had been transferred to Kuala Lumpur!

Kuala Lumpur became so enjoyable to him that he left Young & Rubicam for another agency and eventually was placed in charge of all the Pepsico accounts in the Far East. That included Taco Bell, KFC, and others, and his territory stretched from India to the Philippines. During his tenure in the advertising business he helped his parents move to Canada and purchased property in North Carolina, Canada, and other locations. Sandy eventually retired and bought a home in Bangkok and a condo in Maui, sold the condo, and bought a home in a San Diego suburb. He retains his US citizenship and travels frequently between the Thailand and the United States enjoying the golf courses of both countries.

Sandy's father was English and Chinese and his mother

was Chinese. He was born in Shanghai during the Second World War. The family owned a large textile factory and his father was the Chinese Tennis Champion player in 1949. That was the year Mao Tse Tung became the first leader of the Peoples Republic of China, a post he held until his death in 1976. Mao's socio-political programs such as the Great Leap Forward and the Cultural Revolution would dramatically change the social landscape of China and have a direct effect on Sandy and his family.

Marshal Chen Yi, one of Mao's Grand Military Marshals, had organized a tennis match at an exclusive club. Sandy's father was the premier tennis player in China at the time and was invited to be one of the participants. After the match Yi, who was the equivalent of the Mayor of Shanghai, approached him. Yi had served with Mao on the Long March, an 8,000-mile yearlong trek through some of the most difficult terrain in Western China, and had been rewarded with his current position. The Long March had been the turning point from near annihilation by the army of Chiang Kai-Shek and vaulted Mao Tse Tung into political prominence. Yi later served as Vice Premier and Foreign Minister. He was purged, but not officially dismissed from the Mao régime in 1967.

Sandy's father had been asked play in the tournament. After the match the Mayor, Chen Yi, approached Sandy's father and asked, "Why are you here?" Sandy's father, still in his tennis outfit and perspiring from the match he'd just completed, identified himself. The Mayor said, "You don't belong here," took out a paper and told Sandy's father to list everybody in his family who he would take with him IF he were permitted to leave the country. Yi made it clear that the family was no longer welcome in the new China as their textile mill had already been confiscated. Sandy's father completed the papers, and, while still standing in his tennis garb, watched the official take the paper, review it, and stamp it with his official seal. Shortly thereafter six-year old Sandy was pulled out of school in the middle of the day and taken, with his family to the train depot. The family was permitted to leave and take with them a sum of cash as well as gold bars which were then worth about US$30,000, and a few of their possessions. They packed the allotted items and left the factory and most of their possessions behind, and were ushered aboard a train to Hong Kong, where they remained as refugees for the next 18 months. They stayed at the old Kowloon Hotel, located across the street from the famous Peninsula Hotel. Sandy's father spent his time applying for visas to gain entry to another country. He made repeated requests for entry visas to the USA, Peru, and several European countries where they had friends or contacts from the early days, but were rejected by all. Finally, after a year and a half of waiting, Peru was the first and only country to offer them a visa.

Peru was an excellent choice to relocate. Sandy's grandfather had been the Ambassador to Peru two decades earlier and the family had contacts there. Upon their arrival in Lima, Peru they used their cash to set up a decorating and furniture business that thrived. Sandy's father found a tennis club that would become the training location for Sandy to develop his tennis skills, which would eventually see him become a national champion and earn him a full tennis scholarship at Brigham Young University.

LIMA, PERU IN THE ROARING TWENTIES

During the late 1920s and early 1930s, more than a decade before Sandy's birth, a series of events would occur that would impact the lives of Sandy and his family for many years to come. A dashing young American Army Major by the name of Charles Allen was stationed with his wife in Lima. The Major served as the military chargé d'affaires. Major Allen was a handsome, charming, hard drinking gambler married to a wealthy U.S. socialite and daughter of the first Democrat and first Jewish Governor of Utah, Simon Bamberger. Governor Bamberger had come to the U.S. from Germany at age 14, just before the Civil War began. He was headed to Cincinnati where there was said to be a large prosperous German-Jewish community, but he fell asleep aboard the train and missed his connection in Columbus, ending up instead in Terre Haute, Indiana where he spent the rest of the war. After the Civil war ended Simon moved to St. Louis where he and his brother established a clothing business. A bad debt that potentially could have wiped out the business sent Simon to Wyoming in an effort to collect, but the debtor had disappeared, so young Simon continued on to Utah. He dabbled in various businesses including hotel ownership in Ogden and Salt Lake City, silver mines, and the railroad. He built an amusement park, The Lagoon, outside Salt Lake City, that thrives to this day. Simon invested well, particularly in the foundering oil business, and those investments would eventually make him and his descendants very, very wealthy.

His only daughter Dorothy, called Didi, enjoyed the wealth and status as a member of the upper class. She craved adventure and her husband the Major provided it. Many of her family members thought she had "married down" by wedding the charming, handsome career Army man with no prominent family history. The Major was high maintenance, especially with his preference for the good life and assorted gambling activities. And while the Major was a gambler, he did not often win, and his wealthy wife usually picked up his gambling markers. But even the wealthy have their limits.

During a stint in Lima, Peru the Major continued to gamble and the markers continued to accrue. When the marker tally was completed after a series of losses, the Major owed about $35,000 (which by today's value would be near a half million dollars). Didi refused to pay the markers and the club threatened to arrest the Major if he was unwilling or unable to pay his gambling markers.

The Major pleaded with his wife to pay the markers for if he were arrested his career as an up-and-coming Army officer would be over. Didi did not want to give in but neither did she want to see her husband disgraced and have his career ruined so she turned to the only person she thought might be able to help. She phoned her friend, the Chinese Ambassador (Sandy's grandfather) and asked if there was anything that could be done to minimize the debt. Even with her wealth she would be hard pressed to cover the vast amount of his losses. The Ambassador said he would do his best to try to negotiate a settlement. The Ambassador went directly to the President of Peru and pointed out that to arrest an American Military chargé d'affaires for a gambling debt was bad politics and would indeed be a sticky wicket that would cause a huge embarrassment not only to the Major, but to the U.S. Army and to the government of Peru. The president contacted the owners of the club and together they agreed to settle the debt for about 20 percent of what was owed.

Didi paid the negotiated amount—about $7,000 ($100,000 by today's monetary standards) and thanked her friend the Ambassador profusely. Each time they met thereafter Didi reminded him, "If there is ever anything I could do to return the favor, please let me know."

FROM CHAOS COMES
OPPORTUNITY

After Sandy's family left China, the decision by the
Peruvian government to grant an entry visa to the
family who had lived through a tumultuous 18 months in
Hong Kong, was met with joy and relief. The post-war revolution in China would eventually displace millions and the
world was living through the post-World War resettlement
of millions of displaced European Jews, ex-Nazis, and other
homeless persons (referred to as D P's or Displaced Persons).
The countries of the world were mostly economically deci-
mated from the War and did not have the appetite for more
refugees who generally arrived with little besides the clothes
on their backs. The United States, whose economy was on
the upswing after World War II and had stimulated their
middle class, had harsh limits on the number of immigrants
it would accept. Thus, when Peru, Sandy's family's last best

hope, finally granted the family entry visas it was the first step in rebuilding their lives.

Upon arriving in Lima, Sandy's grandfather used his personal and business contacts that had been made decades earlier and the money and gold he had left after spending 18 months in a Hong Kong hotel, to become a prominent businessman in Lima. Sandy's father went into the business as well as becoming a respected tennis player at Lima's prestigious Miraflores Country Club. Sandy followed in his father and grandfather's athletic footsteps and became an outstanding tennis player in his own right, becoming the National Junior Tennis Champion of Peru two years running as a high school lad.

Nearly three decades after the gambling debt negotiation had been completed it came time for Sandy to attend college. His grandfather contacted Didi, with whom he had maintained a friendship since their days together in Peru, and told her of Sandy's accomplishments on the court. He then asked if she had any thoughts of where he might use those tennis skills play for a good college in the United States. Didi went to her brother Clarence, by then the family patriarch, and posed the question to him. Clarence contacted his friend Dave Freed, Captain of the U.S. Davis Club team, who was from Utah and knew most of the collegiate tennis coaches. Freed made a few calls and based on Sandy's strong tennis resume, a full tennis scholarship was offered to him by the BYU coaching staff. Thus, Sandy and I, both with backgrounds as different from the main as they were different from one another, became next-door neighbors in a BYU dormitory. We were so different in so many ways but shared a bond of being irresponsible 17-year old free thinkers and slobs in the midst of a highly structured, conservative, everything-in-its-place Mormon university environment.

Sandy had come from an international culture and was much better versed on world affairs and world geography than was I. It was difficult going from an upper class living environment in Latin America to a dormitory lifestyle of mostly Mormon college kids who had no clue of life outside their enclave. I had similar difficulty adjusting, but not for the same reasons. In a sense I had been pampered too, as the only son in an ethnic family, but certainly not because of any worldly culture in my background. Nevertheless, Sandy and I had more commonalities than differences. Neither of us were Mormons and both felt out of place. We became fast friends and that friendship has lasted a lifetime.

SEVERE FOOD POISONING:

The dorms were nearly new—they had only opened the previous school year so we were just the second residents of our dorm room. Each room was a mirror image of the others, and each had two sleeping beds against opposite walls. At the head of the bed was a desk and bookshelves attached to the wall above the desk. A fluorescent light mounted below the bookshelves provided light for reading at the desk or in bed. Every room had a telephone with free campus and local calls but no long distance service unless the charges were reversed, although incoming long distance calls could be received. On the outside wall between the two desks was a locking push-out window for ventilation in the warmer months. At the foot to each bed were a built-in set of drawers below a door with a mirror on one side and built-in shelves for toiletries on the other, and a tall closet for hanging clothes. The rooms were nice but Spartan. Each dorm was three stories tall with two wings. In the center of the bottom floor was the apartment of the on-site dorm mother, Sister Jean May, as well as a study area, lounge, and milk and snack vending machines.

Several dorms had been built in a spoke-like semi-circle with Cannon Center, the dining commons in their midst. Also in the dining commons were assigned mailboxes, recreation area, TV room, and the like. The architecture was both efficient and aesthetically appealing.

Parents of dorm residents who lived long distances would often send "care packages" of cookies, meats, and other edible goodies from home. Some of the items were perishable, which presented a problem, as there were no individual refrigerators permitted in any of the rooms. The problem was solved during the long, cold Utah winters by hanging the perishable items on the locking handle of the push-out window. The food would dangle outdoors and stay cold. Outside the window was a ledge about three feet wide and should one so desire, one could squeeze through the open window, walk along the ledge, and inspect the booty that hung outside various windows. There were stories of meats being taken by presumably hungry college men, but for some reason nobody ever took the pungent pepperonis or salamis that my mother sent in the care packages from home.

Sandy had received a Christmas ham from his family. It was fairly large – certainly too large to eat in one or two sittings, so he hung it outside and pulled it in occasionally for late night snacks. As luck would have it we had several warm

Indian Summer days and most dorm residents brought their perishables inside and either ate them or tossed them. Not so Sandy. The ham had been outside for some time, and when I got hungry one evening, crawled out my window and helped myself to a generous portion of the rancid ham.

The following day was to have been a dorm open house so I had made my half of the dorm room neat and orderly, probably for the first time that semester. The bed was made and I slept on top so I would not have to remake it in the morning. I had the keys to a dorm mate's car as I had a breakfast date the following morning, and planned to bring her back to the dorm to show off my room. But sometime that night I remember beginning to shiver. I staggered into the bathroom and began to vomit. Of the rest of the adventure, I have only a foggy memory. I apparently staggered out to the car in my underwear (it was a very cold winter night and had been snowing) and somehow started and drove the car to the Student Health Center on campus. I remember neglecting to close the car door and walking in bare feet through the snow to the emergency entrance. It would be days before I became conscious enough to remember anything more. I had come down with a major case of food poisoning from the ham and spent several days in the infirmary promising myself over and over to never again steal food from anybody!

MAKING MONEY IN THE DORM

O ur particular dorm wing seemed to have an inordi-
nate number of non-Mormons. We often wondered
amongst ourselves if that had been planned to keep an eye
on us and to have us close at hand for proselytizing. Some
of us were less than serious students and others were at the
school because of its academic reputation. Two "gentile" (a
term commonly used for non-members) roommates in the
dorm were from The Bronx, New York. One was named
Benny. They seemed to be much worldlier than the other
non-LDS boys on the floor and they always seemed to be
broke. They constantly tried unconventional methods of
securing for spending money, from hanging a cigar box
(nobody seemed to get the irony of this in a non-smoking
environment) on their door with a note that read, "Feeling
That Financial Squeeze. Please Donate," to finding their

way down into the basement storage room where the dorm residents stored anything and everything of value that would not fit in their dorm room. The Utah boys were a trusting lot and rarely checked up on their property. At year's end when they went to retrieve bicycles, lamps, or just about anything else that could be pawned or sold, and found them missing, Benny and his roommate were long gone back to the Bronx and there was no actual proof that they had been the culprits.

Benny had been given the moniker "the leech" for his constant begging. He and his roommate discovered another interesting way to literally make money. They collected pennies, mostly donations from the box on their door. Pennies have a small ridge around the edge and somehow the boys from the Bronx discovered that by filing the ridge off then filing a little from the face and the tail of the penny, it would become roughly the size and shape of a dime. Of course, nobody, not even the most naïve country bumpkin from Utah would confuse a filed down penny for a dime, but the vending machines would.

Vending machines in the lounge area of each dorm, as well as those in the dining center commons dispensed milk and snacks. Each item cost a nickel so if a person inserted a dime, he would get a product as well as a nickel change. I'm not sure how long the scam worked but many is the night that the Boys from the Bronx circulated amongst all the dorm study areas selling milk and snacks two for the price of one. The scam continued undetected, or at least unsolved, until the end of the school year. Campus Security only figured it out after Benny's dorm room had been vacated and the cleanup crew reportedly walked into a room that was nearly ankle deep in copper dust.

MORE THAN CLASSES

A college education is usually considered to be that which is learned in textbooks, labs, and lectures. But most of what I learned in college came from outside the classroom. There was the Mormon culture of Utah, which was so different from the ethnic, melting pot culture in which I had grown up. There were the trips back and forth between Pennsylvania and Utah during which I met so many Americans. I traveled using all manner of transportation from driving a car, to riding the Big Dog (Greyhound bus), to taking the train to hitchhiking. The trips were usually leisurvely and I often stopped along the way to meet locals.

On one driving trip during the early morning hours in Kansas my eye caught a vehicle driving erratically through mud bogs. I pulled up and stopped the car to get a better view. The vehicle being driven was less of a car and more of a chassis and motor (the forerunner of dune buggies). A couple of boys about my age were just driving through mud puddles having fun. They let me take a few spins and we chatted probably for the better part of an hour. Then one looked at the sun high in the sky and said, "Well, we gotta get hayin' now." I looked confused and he added, "Gotta make hay while the sun shines." They parked their buggy and off they went to do work the fields of their farm.

THE AMAZING MRS.
CHARLES "DIDI" ALLEN

Another component of my education came courtesy of my next-door dorm mate Sandy, who came to BYU on a full tennis scholarship. However, Sandy was not what one might call a gung-ho athlete, the kind who relishes practice and follows the strict regimen required of all BYU athletes, including tennis players. He could not understand why, since he was the best individual player on the team, he was not ranked #1 on the team. He could not grasp the concept of seniority and work ethic, mandatory team study hall. He had the natural athletic ability—which he proved in practice— to defeat any other player on the team. The coach did not appreciate the analysis from a foreign, non-LDS, uppity freshman and they had words with one another. Those words led to his either his quitting or being dismissed from the team. In either event shortly after his college tennis career began, it ended and he had plenty of free time to visit his family friend, Mrs. Dorothy "Didi" Allen.

Sandy and I spent lots of time together and I was fascinated at his knowledge of world history and politics. He was also much better versed in American history and geography than was I. Our conversations about life, politics, cultures, and so many other topics were much more fascinating than most courses I took. Once again I was learning through my ears.

On weekends Sandy would visit the home of Mrs. Didi Allen, the wealthy Jewish woman in Salt Lake City who had helped arrange his admission into Brigham Young University. Now elderly (at least she seemed elderly to a lad of 17. She was in fact probably in her 60s at the time) and a widow who lived on a 30+ acre estate called "Green Acres," that was located on the outskirts of Salt Lake City. As a member of the idle rich she had an onsite butler-chauffer-gardener-handyman who lived with his wife and young son in a separate house on the grounds. The family was from Mexico and although his given name was Jesus (Hay-suse), Mrs. Allen called him "Joey."

In addition to Jesus and his family, Didi employed two fulltime maids, both named Ann. They were referred to as Ann and Ann2. Her staff further included a full time cook, Mrs. Leather, and Arnold, an on-call butler and bartender who looked and acted the part of the proper British butler.

Mrs. Allen was an interesting looking woman, barely five feet in height and less than 100 lbs., long red hair that extended to her waist, ice blue eyes, and a cigarette either in her fingers or in her heavily lipsticked mouth during her every waking moment. The years of smoking had apparently not affected her lungs, as she lived well into her 90s without any respiratory issues, but cigarettes had taken their toll on her skin. When we first met though she was barely into her sixties her wrinkled skin and prune lines on her face created the countenance of an eighty-year old.

Didi was also nearly deaf but refused to wear a hearing device of any kind. She had a special speaker constructed and wired from the television to her favorite TV watching chair. It resembled a lamp with a flexible gooseneck, but instead of a bulb at the end of the gooseneck there was a speaker, much like one from a drive-in movie, in which the volume could be adjusted. Whenever she spoke she shouted and in response one needed to shout back at her lest she not hear.

One week Sandy invited me to accompany him on his regular weekend soiree to Green Acres. I was overwhelmed when we approached the property. I had never been on an estate before. The grounds were like some of the smaller college campuses I had seen in Pennsylvania and included a guest cottage, an Olympic-size swimming pool complete with men's and women's changing and rest rooms, a guest house and in addition to the guest house, and a gigantic cat pen in which she kept dozens of stray cats, properly fed and medicated as dictated by their personal veterinarian who made regular visits to the house. Inside the main house, which was the closest thing to a Southern plantation mansion I had ever seen, lived another half dozen or so cats and at least three dogs. Mrs. Allen might have been a tiny woman but she had a huge heart, especially when it came to helpless animals.

Also part the "Green Acres" estate was a seven-car garage; a converted barn, to accommodate her seven cars—two Cadillacs, a station wagon, a Jaguar, and three other cars. In addition there was a smaller shed that housed two pickup trucks and a tractor. "Joey" kept all the vehicles washed and in good running order. A smaller, newer barn was home for three horses which were available for her and guests to ride the trails that weaved through the property.

Sandy and I spent most of our weekend in "his room," which was a guest suite off the kitchen in the main house. It was amazing! The suite consisted of a bedroom with two double beds, a parlor, a bathroom, and a living room complete with the first color TV set I had ever seen. Each table had fresh flowers changed daily and, as in all other rooms, and a solid silver container that accommodated probably a half carton of cigarettes. We were served breakfast in the suite and took our noon meal at the pool, or in the suite, or in the kitchen, or anywhere we chose. I felt like some sort of aristocrat. This life was 2,000 miles and a world away from the one in which I had grown up in Clairton, Pennsylvania.

On Sunday many of the non-Mormon movers and shakers in Salt Lake City and noted visitors, as well as some open-minded Mormons, would gather for a weekly evening of mirth, food, and drink. It was, I am sure, Mrs. Allen's best replication of Colonial Hong Kong. Dinner would be served then the men would gather in small groups to smoke fine cigars and sip after-dinner Brandy and other drinks while discussing the issues of the world. The women would sit in small groups, drinking and playing cards.

Mrs. Allen was clearly on the international "A" Social List and when people of celebrity came to Salt Lake to ski or for any other purpose, an evening at one of her famous parties was a must stop. Her guest list during my era of visits included boxer Jack Dempsey, actors Hugh O'Brian and Gene Tierney, The Duke and Duchess of Windsor, and countless other celebrities from stage, screen, athletics, the political world, and Captains of Industry most of whose names have faded from my memory over the years.

Mrs. Allen was a collector. She collected fine things, of course, but also collected stray animals and people. Several characters came to her home to visit and never left. One such character was Colonel Charles Sweeny; founding member of the WWII American led Eagle Squadron that was modeled after the Lafayette Escadrille of volunteers and based in Europe. Born in the late 1800s Colonel Sweeny had been named a General in the Polish army and was a close friend of Ernest Hemmingway, Winston Churchill, and Major Charles Allen. Because he was a friend of Major Allen (Didi's late husband) Colonel Sweeny came to the funeral of Major Allen and stayed on until the Colonel passed away some 25 years later!

Colonel Sweeny was extremely well read, especially in

the area philosophy including Kant, Hegel and others. The Colonel was also a bit of a curmudgeon with a bad temper, and did not suffer fools easily. His definition of fools included nearly everyone but himself. Colonel Charles Sweeny was a World War I Army veteran and his passion was to assist with the Lafayette Escadrille, a rag tag group of excellent fliers whom, it was believed, were the primary reason the air superiority of Germany was overcome.

A Time Magazine article describes Col. Sweeny and the Eagle Squadron, modeled after the Lafayette Escadrille as follows: "Correspondents last week discovered the beginnings of this war's equivalent of the Lafayette Escadrille, which in 1916-18 accounted for the high (then) total of 199 German planes. World War II's escadrille is the American Eagle Squadron, quietly recruited and energized by Colonel Charles Sweeney, a U. S. soldier of fortune who fought in the Foreign Legion last time. Both coasts of the U. S. and Canadian-border immigration men had inklings of Colonel Sweeney's missionary work months ago. Last week U. S. newshawks "somewhere in west England" saw two score of his protégés training in yellow-bodied Miles Master planes, almost ready to fly at the throats of the Luftwaffe. They will be ready to do so in a few weeks, when they have graduated. Then they will fly Spitfires and Hurricanes.

"The British made Colonel Sweeny a reserve captain in R. A. F. to make it all pukka. They segregated the reckless Americans, rather than salt them into the conservative R. A. F. Among them are barnstormers, crop-dusters, stunt fliers, sportsmen. Youngest is Gregory ("Gus") Daymond, 19, of California, who used to fly an ice-cream king around South America. Oldest is Paul Joseph Haaren, 48, also of California, a movie flier. Most celebrated Eagle is Colonel Sweeney's nephew, wavy-haired Robert ("Bob") Sweeney, who won the British amateur golf championship in 1937 and lately squired Barbara Hutton Haugwitz-Reventlow. Active commander is Squadron Leader William Erwin Gibson Taylor, 35, formerly of the 5th Fighting Squadron, U. S. Naval Air Corps (aboard the carrier Lexington). He joined Britain's Fleet Air Arm last year, served on the carriers Argus, Furious, and Glorious (sunk at Narvik). Most piquant Eagle name: Harry La Guardia of Hartford, Conn. (no kin to New York City's Mayor).

"Correspondents who interviewed the Eagles at their training field were curious to find out what caused them to join up. Most of the Eagles began their replies by saying, "Well, what the hell?"

Colonel Sweeny continued to recruit American pilots through the early Hitler years. He was threatened with the loss of his U.S. Citizenship for his recruiting of pilots because it was in violation of American Neutrality Laws. But Colonel Sweeny had a strong conviction that Hitler must be stopped so he continued to recruit even with the FBI hot on his trail. He was a remarkable and brave man!

Charles Sweeny, nephew of Colonel Charles Sweeny described his uncle as, "...a well-heeled socialite and businessman living in London." He and his rich society contacts, most likely including Mrs. Allen, bore the cost (over $100,000) of processing and bringing the US trainees to the United Kingdom.

SPANISH NOBILITY?

Another couple that had come to visit Didi and stayed on for years was Mr. and Mrs. Enrique de la Casa. They claimed to be Spanish personas non grata that had been exiled from Spain by the despot, Francisco Franco. Further, they claimed to be lesser Spanish nobility. Enrique was in his 70s and considerably older than his bride who was no spring chicken. The couple reminded me a bit of Juan and Evita Peron. She was pretty but he was tall, thin, and gaunt with a receding hairline and thick wire-rim glasses. His English was very poor, as were his teeth, and he had a habit of shelling and eating heavily salted peanuts while talking. Thus, his most notable characteristic was spitting on his audience as he spoke and chewed his peanuts. He was a most obnoxious man. Didi's brother, Clarence Bamberger, who had both money and political connections, was able to help Enrique get a teaching position in the Spanish Department at the

University of Utah although he was reportedly a horrible teacher.

Maria de la Casa, Enrique's wife, was much younger than her husband, perhaps in her mid 40s. She was attractive in a European sort of way, but had zero personality and was one of the most aloof persons in the group, especially at social gatherings. She rarely had anything of consequence to say and certainly did not contribute to any intellectual conversations. But intellectual stimulation was not the purpose she served in the Green Acres menagerie. Maria was a constant companion to Didi, and served as her personal toady.

Colonel Sweeney considered nearly everybody a fool, with the possible exception of his benefactor, Didi. He had particular disdain for the de la Casas. He considered Enrique not only a fool but also a buffoon without common graces. He considered Maria a whining dolt and little more than a handmaiden to her benefactor, which was to my observation, an accurate assessment. The de la Casas, of course considered the Colonel a freeloading arrogant pompous ass that they despised and made no secret of their feelings toward him.

Other characters that drifted in and out of Didi's life during our college years included Maria Noble and husband Blaine, a postman. Maria Noble, like Didi, was an advocate of the humane society and Blaine was just happy to be in the glorious surroundings that were Green Acres.

Al Buranic was another occasional drop-in. Of his connection with Didi I am not certain, aside from the fact that his wife's mission in life seemed to be to entertain Didi by taking her money in frequent card games. Didi's two constants were smoking and playing cards. The latter provided income to anybody who she could convince to join her in a card game for money. I often wondered if Didi was that bad a card player, or was so starved for company and attention that she lost on purpose.

Didi's cast of characters included intellectuals from Spain, an artist from France, gypsies, tramps and thieves, but nearly all purported to be "very upper class, you know." Her life seemed to be the perfect setting for an F. Scott Fitzgerald novel.

In June of 1961, after the conclusion of our freshman year Sandy went home to Peru for the summer and I stayed in Provo. Mrs. Allen invited me up for the weekend. I hitch-hiked from Provo to her home and to show my gratitude for the invitation I washed all her cars and offered to be a valet car parker for her Sunday guests. She was very impressed at my initiative and Monday morning when I got ready to leave, she handed me a $20 bill. I was ecstatic and at her invitation returned each weekend for the balance of the summer. I earned a bit of spending money and watched and learned. The experience at Green Acres certainly yielded the most I learned about culture and life while in college. Where else could a boy from Clairton, Pennsylvania be exposed to society's upper crust as well as the pretenders? The experience was the beginning of my metamorphosis from kid from a steel town on the river to young adult who appreciates the differences among people. I learned to be tolerant and understanding. Those I believed to be so far above my social status as to be intimidating were themselves full of self-doubts and insecurities. The experience could have easily given me graduate credit in my major field of Psychology.

FRESHMAN YEAR EPILOGUE

Freshman year was also a time to bump into things, figuratively speaking, and occasionally run afoul of the BYU establishment. One such incident occurred early in the semester and was the result of Sandy's desire to spruce up his dull, drab, dorm room that looked like my dull drab dorm room and that of everybody else in the dorm. Sandy's roommate, Lonnie Carter, was an African American from Houston, Texas. Neither Lonnie, nor Sandy, nor I were content living in little boxes made of ticky-tacky that all looked just the same. We made a pact to look for something that would jazz up the place. One evening after heading to downtown Provo for a dinner out we (Sandy, a friend, and I) were driving back to the dorms. As we drove past the rear of a Safeway grocery store Sandy shouted for the friend to stop the car and back up. There among the trash were several aluminum barrels, small enough to work as support for a tabletop piece of plywood. We tossed the mini-barrel into the trunk along with some plywood that lay nearby, and within an hour Sandy and Lonnie had the spiffiest study table in the dorm.

One of the other non-Mormons on the floor was Benny the Leech from the Bronx. He had a habit of never paying his way regardless of the circumstance. In fact, when we would go as a group to the snack bar at the nearby bowling alley, Benny would always eat but never pay. He earned his nickname, "Benny the Leech" at the snack bar when somebody ordered a burger and fries and reached for the catsup. Benny stopped him saying, "No! I don't like catsup on my fries."

Benny came to the room to see the now-famous table, lifted up the skirt draped over the plywood and said, "Hey, where'd you get the cool beer keg?" Up to that point nobody in the dorm realized what the stand actually was. At least nobody had the gall to say it aloud. And of course, Sandy answered with the wide-eyed innocence of a naïve teen when he said, "I found it."

What happened next is speculation, but the logical sequence of events would be that a dorm official would have heard about the keg and entered Sandy's room with a passkey, written the identification number stamped on the keg, and then phoned campus security who in turn phoned the Provo Police. Once it was discovered that the keg had been "stolen" from a downtown Safeway market, the Barney Fyfe Serious Crimes Unit of the Provo Police Department swung into action. They confiscated the "evidence" while most students were away from the dorm and awaited Sandy's return. As he walked into the dorm, two burly plainclothesmen approached him, asked his name, and slapped the cuffs on him. They escorted him to their unmarked patrol car and took him to the station for questioning.

The next several hours must have seemed like an eternity to the terrified lad, alone and far from home. Detectives had him write a statement then grilled him about being part of a ring that was stealing beer kegs, and told him that such a theft could be a felony that would land him in jail until long after his classmates were gone from school and in their careers. They insisted he tell them who else was in the beer keg theft ring and generally terrorized poor Sandy.

But Sandy refused to stray from his original story. He was driving home from dinner (What are the names of the other gang members who were with you?) There is no gang. I saw a pile of trash in the back of the store and thought the keg would make a good study table base. (Why didn't you ask the store manager for permission to take it?) The store was closed. (Why would you take an item that costs lots of money and is reused for years?) I thought it was trash. I've never seen a beer keg before. I'm from Peru. I did not know they were reused.

Eventually the interrogation ceased and the Keystone Kops released Sandy with a severe warning that he was being watched and any further law breaking would be dealt with harshly.

THE ACCIDENTAL
LIBRARIAN

As the school year came to a close and my parents agreed that I could stay on for summer school, I decided that I was in need of a job, so I went to the campus placement office and saw an ad for a part time worker in the campus library. Because the library was a building with which I had little familiarity I decided it might be something interesting, so I applied. A tall statuesque woman named Grace Allphin interviewed me, and our 15-minute interview turned into a two-hour conversation. She told me about her huge family (ten children; five girls, five boys), her husband, and her sons, several of whom played football for BYU and served missions for the church. I told her about Clairton and my accidental trek from the steel mills of Pennsylvania to the mountains of Utah. She said that every young man away from home needed a good home cooked meal and invited me to her house for dinner. Sister Allphin became my surrogate mother at Brigham Young University and, oh yes, she hired me on the spot.

It is difficult to imagine the profound influence the Allphin family had on my development as a still-raw 18-year old. Two of their daughters, Jessie, #5 and Marilyn, #6 were about my age and I'd often see them on campus. Jessie was shy and studious, Marilyn more outgoing. Both pursued careers in education, Marilyn finished a PhD degree, and Jessie became a school superintendent. Their brothers were also terrific role models and they treated me as an extended family member. I shared their laughter and cried with them when a brother, Harold, met a tragic end. We eventually lost touch with each other and it was only recently that I learned that Grace had passed away too soon as the result of an error during a surgical procedure.

Grace Allphin was much more than a boss to me. She was not only tall and confident, but the essence of a super-mom. She and husband Nylen not only valued and emphasized education, they lived their philosophy as evidenced by the fact that every one of their ten children attended college, all but Harold, who passed away prematurely, graduated and most earned graduate degrees. The degree count or the Allphin children was as follows: Nine have bachelor's degrees, two have PhDs, and several have master's degrees. In an interview with Dr. Marilyn Allphin Miller she states, "The work ethic was deeply engrained by my father and mother along with careful spending. We learned to consider all members of the family and all of our needs." It was a formula that worked!

The education I received at Mrs. Allen's Sunday parties, rubbing elbows with the rich and famous, was tempered with the time I spent with the Allphin family. They were as real an All American family as could be described.

The BYU library collection was housed in the Grant Building, and had been for decades. It was a closed stack library meaning that if one wanted to check out a book he completed a form with the required information and took it to a desk where a librarian would enter the catacombs of stacks to retrieve it. Only library employees were permitted in the stacks of the collection that included some 30,000 books. A new library that had a capacity to house a million books was about to open that summer and part of my duties included packaging up books to be moved from the Grant Library to their new dwelling. During the time the collection was being moved the large, five story new library, which included two levels underground and three above and operated as a closed stack library. That meant, if a student came to the desk needing several books, I might have to run from floor one to floor five to retrieve them. That summer I was as fit as I've ever been before or since. The experience also gave me the opportunity to learn the huge library and its collection intimately. My duties included an hour or so each day "reading the shelves," which meant I would scan the shelves to locate books that had been misfiled, for if a book was out of place it was essentially lost to the collection. I so enjoyed my time working in the library that I began taking Library Science courses and completed a Library Science endorsement as one of my several minor fields of study.

My duties in the library expanded once the new building was opened. The school had invested in a brand new high-tech machine that promised to eliminate the need for carbon paper. Until that time, whenever a paper for a class assignment was typed, carbon paper was slipped between the sheets in order to make multiple copies. This new contraption was able to accept a sheet of paper on a glass, have it covered, and with the press of a button, a perfect replica would result – or two or three or however many were desired. This new-fangled machine was called Xerox, and I was one of the first to be trained in its use and maintenance. Of course, maintenance meant clearing paper jams and reloading fresh reams of paper. Otherwise when the machine refused to function, an official, factory-trained representative was needed.

For the most part freshman year was uneventful. Probably the most daring thing we did intentionally was to leave class after roll was called.

FORUM AND DEVOTIONAL

Officials at Brigham Young University worked diligently to provide students with spiritual and educational examples of leadership and good moral examples of life. Every Wednesday at 10:00 a.m. in the Fieldhouse one of two classes was held. On the first and third Wednesday of the month the class was called "Forum," and on the second and fourth Wednesday of the month the class was called, "Devotional." Each class was worth a half-credit. Students who signed up were on their honor to attend, which meant, of course, that Sandy and I and our other immature freshman friends would usually cut the class. The last day of class a computer punch card was given to each attendee and marked as to the number of classes that had been missed. Attendance of 80 percent or more earned half a credit for each course. Anything less and no credit was given. Four half credits (two credits) allowed the student to skip one semester of required Religion courses.

On Forum dates the school brought in nationally and internationally known speakers, not necessarily Mormon, but nearly always conservative political thinkers. Examples included conservative news commentators Paul Harvey and William F. Buckley, Jr. and Senator Barry Goldwater. Devotional speakers were generally highly placed church officials or other noted Latter Day Saint speakers such as Steven Covey and Bill Marriott. It was an excellent forum but a little too mature for my gang and the result was many missed academic opportunities to hear outstanding speakers.

The same Fieldhouse served as the basketball arena as well as a venue for entertainment. Some of the entertainment was a bit edgy for 1960 BYU. One example was a concert that featured the folk singing group Peter, Paul, and Mary, one of the most popular groups in America at the time. The group came onto the stage and when the applause quieted one member said, "My name is Peter, but I'm not an apostle." The crowd laughed and applauded.

Next, "My name is Paul, but I'm not an apostle." The crowd clapped and chuckled.

Third came the female vocalist who said, "My name is Mary...." The implication that she was not a virgin and would announce it on stage brought the crowd to its feet. Remember, this was Provo, Utah in 1960, not New York City!

Thus ended my freshman year at BYU.

MY HIGH SCHOOL BUDDY GENO

Early on during my freshman year I had several bouts with homesickness. When I would get "down" I would write letters. I think I wrote to everybody I ever knew. For some reason my parents had brought a Clairton telephone directory on the trip to Provo, and left it in my dorm room. I looked up the addresses of as many of my former classmates and buddies as I could find, then bombarded them as well as my sisters, parents, and every shirttail relative, with letters. I wove tales about the beauty of Utah and pressed every one of my high school buddies to consider joining me at BYU. I even had the Admissions office send scads of applications and school information to my hapless friends across the country. One friend, Geno Tolari, took the bait and asked me to send him a second application, which I did. I also sent letters regularly, telling about what a great time I was having.

In one such letter I included a copy of the newspaper article that had been published with my name attached. It had been submitted to the newspaper by my English teacher Mrs. McKay and was a story about Clairton. In the article I joked about several of the less glamorous parts of the community. It was meant to be a satire.

Geno was impressed and showed the article to his mother who showed it to a friend, and it eventually reached the office of the Mayor, who promptly called my father, a city worker, on the carpet. The Mayor railed about how my father's son was making a mockery of our town and he wondered how my father, a City employee, could tolerate such demeaning behavior toward our lovely city. That night the phone lines between Clairton and Provo were on fire with colorful language and my father let me know that I had "made a fool out of him" (one of his favorite expressions when he was feeling put upon) and reminded me that I was there to get an education, not make fun of the city where I had grown up. His point was well taken. That ended my career, albeit temporarily, as a writer of newspaper articles about my old hometown. Ironically, 50 years later I began publishing a blog under the title Olio and the pseudonym of Dr. Forgot. Most of my blog posts are about my hometown as it is and as it once was, and of the many Clairtonians who have left town to make an impact on the world. The blog can be located at *http://drforgot.blogspot.com*.

Geno had been a much better student than I in high school and because he was Catholic, his father was pushing him to attend Duquesne University, a Catholic school in downtown Pittsburgh. Geno wanted to get away from home. One evening during a heated discussion about college, Geno said to his Dad, "Oh, yeah? Well maybe I'll go out to Utah and attend school with the Mormons!"

His Dad spoke the rejoinder common in those days, "Well don't let the door hit you on the ass on the way out," as he stomped out of the room. In an act of defiance, Geno completed the admissions application packet and began to plan for college in Utah.

By the time my freshman year had ended, my roommate Phil Ruiz was ecstatic to be rid of me. He moved out and Geno moved in that September 1961. Fortunately for the both of us, neither Geno nor I were meticulous about our personal housekeeping habits, so a sloppy room did not bother either of us. I had matured a little after my freshman year in some ways but not in terms of my housekeeping.

Every student at Brigham Young University was required to take a two-credit course in religion each semester. During my freshman year I'd taken Bible Studies, but the rules had changed and as of 1961 incoming freshmen were required to take a Book of Mormon class. Geno and I signed up to take the class together and I must admit (as would Geno) that he did not study much that year. When we had our first Book of Mormon course exam we sat next to one another and since I had superior knowledge, having gone through the missionaries indoctrination my freshman year, the exam questions were not difficult for me. Geno, however, needed a little assistance, which he got by looking at my paper.

A few days later we both received notification letters to attend a meeting of the Honor Council in reference to possible cheating on an exam. Our meeting times were scheduled back to back. Keep in mind that by my second year I had learned to "play the game" and was easily able to mask the cocky Clairton city-kid attitude when necessary. Geno, not so much. My meeting was first and it went as follows:

"Good morning, Brother Nixon."

"Good morning Brother (whatever his name was)"

"I'll cut to the chase. Were you cheating on your Book of Mormon exam?"

"Oh no sir, I would not cheat."

"Did you notice anybody looking at your paper?"

"Actually, Brother, I did not pay attention to anybody but myself. I took the exam and left the room."

"Thank you, Brother Nixon. That will be all." And I left the office, winking at Geno on the way out. Later that day he reviewed with me the essence of his interview with the Honor Council member. It went as follows:

"Good morning, Brother Tolairi."

"First, Jack, it's Tolari, not Tolairi. Second, I ain't your brother."

The young man was taken aback and tried to recover. "Very well, *Mr.* Tolari. Why were you cheating on your Book of Mormon test?

"I didn't cheat."

"It will be better for you if you were truthful."

"Look, Jack, two things I hate are cheaters and liars. You

just accused me of being both. If you accuse me of one more thing I didn't do, I'll whip your ass right here on the spot."

"Uhh, ahhh, mmm, Brother, er, Mr. Tolari, we will give you a break on this one since it is your first, uh, appearance here."

Geno, sensing the smell of blood knew he had the little fella on the ropes and pressed his victory, "You ain't giving me a break cuz I didn't do nothing…"

And so it went. He won the battle but would not win the war. The campus security force had their eyes on Geno, and by extension on me, his roommate. They would stop us on campus if we rode a bike and say they had received a report of a stolen bike, then hassle us before letting us go. Since they never actually discovered anything illegal, Geno relished in beating them and challenged them to their face. I was not so bold.

IN NEED OF A SET OF WHEELS

Geno and I decided we needed a car. One of our dorm mates, Sid Hobb, had an uncle who was a farmer north of Salt Lake City who had an old car in his barn. The car had not been driven in years but he'd probably sell it. Our dorm mate didn't know the make or whether or not the car was in running condition but he assured us the price would be right so one weekend Sid drove his car and he, Geno, another friend Jim Tolley, who knew about cars, and I went up to look at the chariot that was for sale. The car was a 14-year old stick shift Packard, big as a tank, which had been sitting in the barn with hay strewn over it. The battery was dead, the tires were bald, and the overdrive switch was broken, but once we got it started it purred like a kitten and Jim pronounced it "solid as a rock." We asked how much he wanted for it and the farmer said $80. We each had $20 in our pockets so the farmer agreed we could take the car with the $40 down payment if we promised to send him the balance within a month. We agreed and drove off in our mutually owned car. One month later we each gave $20 to Sid who personally delivered it to his uncle.

Jim Tolley was able to climb under the car and use a cable to release the overdrive setting so we were able to push start the car despite it having a very dead battery. The bald tires looked as if they might not last through the winter but our first order of business was a new battery. Upon arriving in Provo we cruised the downtown area until Geno directed me to pull into a parking space next to a brand new Buick. He explained that the Buick and the Packard used similar batteries. He popped the hood on the Buick and, in a trice the batteries were switched. We had a new battery, but I expressed a concern that a sweet little old lady might be the owner of the Buick would be left with a dead battery. He rolled his eyes as though I was as naïve as the average Utahn and said, "She will call the dealership and they will replace the battery with a new one. Everybody wins!" Sounded logical to my 18-year old ears, so off we went with our bald tires and a new battery. We later discovered a store that sold used recapped tires for $5.00 apiece.

Geno's victory over the Honor Council dweeb was short lived. Once we registered the car on campus and secured a BYU parking sticker, Campus Security saw Geno's name and immediately began to pull us over on a regular basis. Occasionally we would take young ladies up to an area called

"Rock Canyon," Provo's passion pit, to park. The campus saying among boys was "Go up Rock Canyon and get a little boulder." Winters were cold so it was not unusual for students who took dates to the Canyon to bring along blankets to snuggle under while watching submarine races. Upon our return to campus Security would inevitably pull us over, search our car, and write us warnings for "stealing dorm bedding" and the like. Geno had won the battle but the Campus Machine was winning the war.

ACCIDENTS WITH GIRLFRIENDS

Sidney Hobb, whose uncle sold us the Packard, hailed from North Salt Lake City, a working class part of the town. His high school girlfriend was Vicki Vascher, and her best friend was Margie Hughes. Both Vickie and Margie were student nurses and Margie, an only child who had been born in England, owned a powder blue 1952 Chevy. Sid took me home with him one weekend and we double dated. Margie and I hit it off and we dated most of my freshman year. By my sophomore year Sid and Vickie had broken up, Sid had dropped out of school to work, and I fixed Geno up with Margie's best friend and Sid's former girlfriend, Vickie. Of the four of us (Geno, Vickie, Margie, and myself) only Margie had a car. Once we bought the Packard, however, Geno was liberated and spent more time with Vickie than in class. By the end of the school year, Geno had been academically dismissed from BYU, was expecting a baby, and he and Vickie married. I gave him my half interest in the Packard as a wedding present and he completed the rest of his education at the University of Utah in Salt Lake City while he, Vickie, and the baby lived with her parents.

Geno might have been a little rebellious but he was a very intelligent young man who settled into married life and graduated from the University of Utah with honors. He moved his family to Silicon Valley, near San Francisco, and became the CEO of a company that was a major player on the computer component scene. Geno's offbeat manner and personality coupled with his brilliant brain were perfect fits for the young company that had hired him. He and the company thrived and today Geno lives in California on an estate atop a hill that overlooks thousands of acres of unspoiled government land.

Margie and I eventually broke up. She began dating Sidney and they eventually married. One day, after she and Sid had been married for years and had several children, Margie decided the traditional life was not for her. She was a hippie at heart, and left her husband and family to join a commune. She's been rarely heard from since.

FINANCIAL ASSISTANCE

In order to help pay for my college life I scrimped and saved, worked in the library, robbed Peter to pay Paul, received help from my parents, and did creative entrepreneurial activities. Many college students did traditional activities to get through school such as earn scholarships, work, and receive help from parents, but some of my entrepreneurial activities were unique. One of my many revenue-generating schemes was to buy old cars from students for cheap, as they were usually not too well maintained. I tried to always buy for less than $100 with a target of $50. I'd shine them up, go to the junkyard and pick up missing chrome and parts, and usually sell the cars for more than double what I had into them.

Another scheme was to identify students who, like me, did not type. When term papers were due and typing was required, I would put out the word that I could have papers typed for a good price (the going rate was between 5 cents and 15 cents per page). I'd get 12 cents per page from my dorm brothers, then shop the young married girls until I found one who would type for between 6 and 8 cents and pocket the difference. I was always on the lookout for clever ways to help pay for my education.

One evening, instead of studying I was watching the old TV western, Wagon Train. As I watched and imagined myself as the wagon master, I began to hatch an idea. I went to each girl's dorm and put a 3X5 card announcement on the bulletin board that read something like: "Driving home for Christmas Break? Live in the East? Concerned about possible breakdowns and safety, flat tires, or other road hazards? Come to a meeting in the Cannon Center Lobby tomorrow at 7:00 p.m."

Now before you start to wonder about my sanity, since my auto mechanic skills ranged somewhere between nil and zero, my logic was this; many girls attending BYU who lived in the east had nice new cars that Daddy bought them to drive to school. The cars were not only new but also well maintained, so the risk would be minimal. When the group arrived for my meeting I handed out blank 3x5 cards then gave them the following spiel: "I'll take a group of up to 10 cars back east in a caravan. I will ride in the last car in the train and be responsible to repair any problems that occur to any of the cars along the way. We will travel along a specific route so if one lives anywhere between Chicago and Pennsylvania, we would travel safely with me as your guardian." I had gotten an American Automobile Association (AAA) "Triptic" which charted the route down to the last 1/10 of a mile and listed all restaurants, service stations, motels and truck stops along the route. We would all stop at the same places for gas, food, lodging, and rest stops. Each driver could take two additional riders as company for no additional charge. The cost of this "insurance" would be $35 per car. Anybody who was interested was directed to write their name, phone number, year and model of car, and destination on the card and leave it with me. I would then plan the route and call those who I agreed to take. I figured (correctly) that there would be no mechanical problems with the new cars.

Between 15 and 20 girls signed up and I charted a route that would stop at each house and end in Pittsburgh. I chose 10 cars whose owners followed the same route. We reversed the route to return after the holidays. I got a free ride and earned $350. That was enough for room and board or more than enough for tuition and books for two semesters.

I became a little more creative at the end of the school year. In those days there were car delivery services. The cost of shipping cars by common carrier must have been prohibitive. Many people who moved across the country, or who spent winters in warmer states had their cars delivered by delivery services. Cars were usually new and big, like our Packard. The Delivery Service Broker would pay for gas, lodging, a nominal fee. The driver had about a week to get the car to its destination. I arranged to drive two cars from Salt Lake City to the Pittsburgh area, then posted a card on the "ride board" offering a ride to points east for $25, a huge savings over other modes of transport. I let one person drive the second car for free and packed five passengers into each car and get home for free plus earn a little spending money for the next school year.

OFF TO HAWAII

At some point during my sophomore year my father, who was ecstatic that I was on track for graduation and maintaining a decent grade point average, decided to reward me. He had discovered that BYU had recently begun a campus in Hawaii. The cost of a semester at the Church College of Hawaii, as it was then called (the name was later changed to BYU Pacific) was about the same as the cost of a semester in Provo so it was decided that I would attend my junior year in the sunny climes of Hawaii. The year was 1962 and as the spring semester wore down I met a girl named Beryl who was also planning to attend the Church College of Hawaii in the fall.

Unbeknownst to me, Beryl's father was a high official at the college. Further unbeknownst to me was that the Church College of Hawaii was expanding their athletic programs, particularly tennis and basketball. During our dates I had regaled Beryl with tales of my alleged tennis prowess. I had simply used my buddy Sandy's stories (he was a scholarship player on the BYU tennis team) and substituted my name for his in my tales of adventure, aces, and tennis victories. I even used one of Sandy's favorite expressions to indicate a job well done, "Game, set, match!"

My tales of my tennis superiority so impressed Beryl that she wrote her father to tell him of this wonderful tennis player she had met and who was planning to come to CCH in the fall. One day I received a letter in the mail from the Church College of Hawaii tennis coach offering me a partial scholarship if I would play on their tennis team.

I raced back to the dorm, letter in hand and showed it to Sandy. I asked if he thought I could pull it off and he suggested we go out on the courts and he would assess my actual tennis prowess. It took fewer than 30 minutes (but it seemed like hours to me— all that running and heavy breathing) before he said, "You won't fool anybody. You're hopeless as a tennis player." My athletic prowess to that point had been limited to shifting gears in the Packard, and I'd often grind the gears when shifting. Still, I was so flattered at the scholarship offer, and was even more excited about the possibility of being a varsity. athlete I mean, how many people in Hawaii could play tennis competitively anyhow? Don't they just sail around in those funny canoes, eat at luaus and watch hula-girls? How hard could it be to fool them? Thus I decided to try to fake it, and wrote the coach a letter accepting his offer.

FLASHBACK

I finished my final exams early and bought a bus ticket home to Pennsylvania to see my parents before going to Hawaii but visited only briefly as I was anxious to get back to the west and to Hawaii.

On the bus trip to Pennsylvania and across the country I sat behind two middle-aged women. As I eavesdropped on their conversation I could tell they were anxious. They spoke only Spanish and this was apparently their first bus trip in the U.S. and they were not sure how to get to their destination, New York. I asked, in Spanish, if I could help and they told me they knew nothing of the U.S. but handed me their itinerary. They had gotten on the bus in Denver, and were to change buses in Chicago and Pittsburgh. I told them I would help them and we chatted all the way to Pittsburgh including a change of buses in Chicago. I had taken high school Spanish (4 years of first year Spanish, I tell people) and had practiced the language with Sandy who was reared in Peru.) I was reared in a bilingual household and have an ear for languages. Thus I was able to communicate with the women.

When we disembarked from the bus in Pittsburgh my parents were waiting to take me to Clairton. I brought my two new friends over and introduced them. My parents were bi-lingual, speaking English as well as Serbo-Croatian, but no Spanish, and the two women spoke only Spanish. So as they rattled on in Spanish about what a nice, helpful son my parents had, my mother turned ashen. I took the women to their New York-bound bus and only then, as we drove to Clairton, did my mother tell me that she thought, from listening to their conversation and watching their gestures, that I had married one of them. We had a good laugh and she retold that story for the next 40 years.

Before I left Clairton for Provo and on to Hawaii, my mother told me that my paternal grandfather had phoned and wanted me to stop by and see him. I had rarely seen my paternal grandfather, as he and my father did not get along. My grandmother was bedridden, nearly blind with cataracts, and spoke no English. My grandfather spoke very little. Their house always had a distinctive smell of the ethnic foods they prepared – always heavy on the garlic.

My grandfather, whom we called "Big Diedo" stood about 6'2" and was still built like Adonis, even in his sixties. He was very self sufficient and his house had a cellar where he baked breads and made cheeses, and nearby was an enclosed area where he smoked meat, and a barn whose walls boasted Blue Ribbons and certificates that he proudly displayed. He made other cheese products, grew vegetables, cured tobacco and was indeed a very self-sufficient man. He would have made a good Mountain Man had he settled in Colorado instead of Clairton.

In his broken English he said, "You go college overseas. You good boy. No chase girls like your cousins (if he only knew). I want give you cheese for have food when you go overseas." I'm sure he envisioned me traveling steerage as he had done aboard a smelly ship in 1907 when he first immigrated to America. Then he said "Checkai," the Slavic equivalent of "Wait a minute," and disappeared. He returned with five crisp $20 bills in his hand. "You no tell Daddy or Mama. This for have good time in college overseas."

I was taken aback. A hundred dollars was more than my plane ticket to Hawaii had cost. It was about the cost of a semester's tuition. Not knowing what to say, I said, in his language, "Hvala Bogo," the equivalent of "Thank God." It was a frequently used expression in his culture. He smiled and winked and said, "No hvala Bogo, hvala Diedo." In other words, this was a gift from Grandpa, not any Deity.

PRE-HAWAII SUMMER

Upon my return to Provo I worked full time in the campus library and made every effort to save money for Hawaii. I became as frugal as possible. Because I had no place to sleep and had not arranged for an apartment, I needed to be creative. I discovered the dorms were being restored during the summer due to water damage, so during the day while the workers stripped, repainted and repaired, I sneaked into one of the rooms and left the ground floor window unlocked. After the workday I would sneak into the room through the unlocked window and stay the night for free. When the sun rose I would freshen up in the dorm men's room, which I had all to myself, then take all my belongings and clear out before the workmen arrived. That saved me the price of an apartment for the summer.

Food was another item on which I scrimped that summer. I had been dating a girl named Kathy Jones who lived in nearby Orem. She had a 1956 Rambler and would often let me take it for the day. In the evenings she worked at the snack bar at the Scera Movie Theater in Orem. I hung out with her at work. One of her perks was free food at the refreshment stand so although I did not eat the healthiest meals, my food bill was next to nothing that summer.

As students left for the summer they were often in a rush to sell their cars. I bought a few "beaters" (beats walking), replaced missing chrome, shined them up, and resold them for at least double my investment. My earnings and savings were part of my cache for Hawaii.

I had planned to spend just a week or so with my family before heading back to Provo to work for the rest of the summer, and take a class or two. Then it was to be on to Seattle to see the World's Fair of 1962, and finally, off to Hawaii. I purchased a very cheap ticket on a propeller-driven plane that went from Oakland (near San Francisco), to Burbank (near Los Angeles), and on to Hawaii. The Burbank to Honolulu portion took eight hours as opposed to four hours on a jet, but the price was right.

By summer's end I left Provo with plans to get to Seattle to see the World's Fair of 1962. My ticket to Hawaii had already been purchased but to get to Seattle and see the famous Space Needle that had been erected as the centerpiece of the World Fair, I decided to use my educated thumb. I planned to hitchhike from Provo to San Francisco then on to Seattle. I stood on the edge of town in Provo,, thumb extended, and within a few minutes a burgundy-colored 1960 Oldsmobile stopped. An older couple was in the car and they invited me to ride. They were such nice, cheery people. The husband was a huge bald-headed man and the wife was as sweet as she could be. As we talked, they asked if I were a BYU student and I said yes. They said they just left their son who was on a football scholarship at BYU. He had been on a mission and returned, married, and had their first two grandchildren; "the most beautiful grandchildren in the world." They had another son who had come to BYU on a basketball scholarship but he had returned home to Sacramento and was working in the family business.

I could not believe what I was hearing. I knew the story and asked, "Are you Wayne Shepard's parents?"

They said, "Yes, do you know him?" Wayne was the young man who had had switched roommates. Jim Kimmel had been assigned to be Phil's roommate and Phil ended up with me as a roommate and a year of slovenly Hell. Wayne had gotten very homesick and his parents missed him as well. He was the youngest child. So by Christmas of our freshman year the parents agreed to buy him a brand new Chevy Impala convertible if he would return home. He agreed and returned to Sacramento where he walked on to the basketball team at Feather River Junior College. Here were his parents, giving me a ride to Sacramento. What a small world!

The rest of the ride went by so fast I don't remember much. When I told them my plans for Seattle and Hawaii they became very concerned. The main north-south freeway between Sacramento and Seattle was Interstate 5. Several servicemen had been murdered while hitchhiking on that highway. They made me an offer; if I would come home with them I could work in their business (Keen Window Cleaning). They had contracts to clean offices at night and could always use another hand. I could drive Wayne's car (that Baby Blue new Chevy convertible) and they would keep me at their house for free. When I left for Hawaii they would give me all the wages I had earned so I would have a grubstake for Hawaii.

It was the proverbial "offer I could not refuse." For the next couple of weeks I worked nights, played days, and earned my grubstake for Hawaii. Wayne let me drive his convertible anytime I wanted to. Between cleaning offices at night and playing during the day I learned all about the North Sacramento area and the Feather River Valley.

Some days Wayne and I and another former BYU buddy, Bill Grundy, would explore the Northern California towns of Placerville, and other historical sites. One day we even ventured into Reno, though none of us were of age. We were escorted out of several casinos after telling kindly security guards that we'd left our ID in the car (like they'd never heard that one before). It was a profitable and fun-filled two weeks. Finally the day came and they took me to the Oakland airport. We hugged and I boarded the plane.

GOODBYE CALIFORNIA, HELLO HAWAII

The flight was so inexpensive because it was a charter. In those days, entrepreneurs would often charter a plane then sell the seats and make a profit – much like I did with the delivery cars between Provo and Pittsburgh. Charter flights were the equivalent of today's small regional airlines. They were held to lower standards than scheduled airlines and their fares were not regulated, as were those of the scheduled carriers. Their equipment was often older and less well maintained and the crews were much less formal with passengers. These things were in evidence when our four-engine propeller aircraft took off from the much small-er (than nearby San Francisco) Oakland airport and within a short period of time, developed engine trouble. The plane was able to limp into Burbank on the remaining engines but we had an unscheduled layover while a new (probably just a different) engine replaced the offending one. Of course, as a stupid kid, I had no fear.

During our several hour mechanical layovers as Burbank I became friendly with three fellow travelers, all young men from New York. Their names were (no kidding) Barry, Harry, and Larry. They were a little older than me—grown men by my perception, probably in their mid-20s. We spotted a man in the airport that we thought looked like comedian Jonathan Winters, a very offbeat comic of the day who regularly did the campus tour. His material was so edgy that he had recently spent time in a mental hospital. We dared each other to ask if it was him and finally, I was elected. I approached him and asked, "Excuse me, Sir, my friends want to know if you are Jonathan Winters."

He removed his hat and studied its inside for several moments then said, "It says Jonathan Winters right here in my hat and I didn't steal the son-of-a-bitch, so it must be me." He signed autographs for us and did a little shtick, then said, "Well boys, I better go now. One slip-up and whoosh, back to the funny farm." He was the most famous person I had ever met up to that time except for the bigwigs at Mrs. Allen's parties. The diversion made our wait for the plane repair worth it.

Not many passengers were on the plane and the flight was a long one. Much of the trip was at night and most of the passengers were asleep. I wandered back to the rear of the plane and began talking to the stewardess, as they were then known. She was very, very friendly and before long we were in an embrace under the blankets in the back rows of the plane and joining the mile-high club while Barry, Harry, and Larry from New York slept in the front rows. Ah, those charter flights.

The plane arrived in Honolulu shortly before dawn. The young hula girls who I had imagined would greet the plane, hang a lei on my neck and welcome me with a kiss, must have worked the day shift. We had a big Hawaiian Grandma who greeted us. Oh well. At least the charter flight had been fun. I caught a bus for the 40-mile ride to the Church College of Hawaii campus at Laie.

The next day, I showed up for tennis practice and was given a "CCH Seasider Tennis Team" polo shirt, with the school logo over the heart. The colors were gold and maroon, much like those of University of Southern California, and the icon was of King Kamehameha and two crossed torches. I was so proud. To wear a varsity shirt was titillating to a kid whose only previous involvement in organized athletics was a snowball fight on the BYU campus. The coach told me that the polo shirt was our uniform and I was to be at practice that afternoon. After practice the coach pulled me aside and said, "Son, we made what we call a recruiting mistake with you. We will honor your scholarship for one semester but you do not have to bother to come to practice or any other squad activities."

I had the gall to ask, "Can I keep the shirt?" He rolled his eyes, nodded, and left.

Two things I did plenty of while in Hawaii were spend

time in the ocean and travel to Honolulu. Two things I did not do much of during my semester in Hawaii were study and attend class. As a result, my grade point average for that semester was 1.17 (very slightly above a D). But oh what a time I had!

Shortly before the semester in Hawaii ended, I celebrated my twentieth birthday. That meant I could get a Hawaii drivers license. The woman at the Hawaii Department of Motor Vehicles was kindly and since I passed the written test, did not require a driving test (since I had hitch-hiked to the DMV as I did not have a car). She said, "Since you just turned 20, that will be your birthday present."

My Hawaii driver's license, which I still have, has no expiration date on it. A few years ago I was consulting in Hawaii every couple of weeks. I rented from Budget Rentacar and got to know the staff at the airport kiosk. They would often give me the "kamaaina" rate, for locals, or upgrade my car to a convertible. One day I brought my 1963 drivers license and presented it to the employee who I'd gotten to know. She got a big kick out of it, but still required my home state license.

Over the years I have decided that unless you are independently wealthy the best way to enjoy Hawaii is to be young, stupid, and without responsibility. That is how I enjoyed it.

My semester in Hawaii was most enjoyable if not academically disastrous. Much of my time was spent on the beach, walking distance from campus. The student body was made up of about 80 percent non-whites including native

Hawaiians, Japanese, Chinese, Filipinos, Samoans, Tongans, and other South Sea islanders. It was a tremendous cultural experience, despite my grade point average. It was a great lesson of how it felt to be a minority. I stayed just one semester but had the time of my life.

I became friends with two young ladies, Helene Myers and Sally (Sueko) Takahashi, both locals, both of Japanese ancestry, and both taught English at the college. Sally invited me to visit her family home on the Big Island of Hawaii over Christmas vacation. Her family lived in the village of Hawi, on the northern tip of the island. For the two weeks I visited, I did not see another haole (white person). I met her mother, who had been treated roughly by American soldiers during World War II, as she washed their clothes while nursing a broken arm. My time in Hawaii was only two decades since the attack on Pearl Harbor, and many Japanese Americans still had the bitter taste of war in their mouths. I met Sally's sister and brother-in-law, Kamalo and Hanako Yamamoto. He had such a laid back attitude toward life. He would fish and the family would dine on whatever he caught. It was another valuable learning experience for me, and a time to see people as who they were rather than as stereotypes.

One of my dorm mates had an old Harley Davidson motorcycle and he would let me drive it to "town," as Honolulu was called. The bike was a "64" model and had a gear shift aside the gas tank. It was an oldie, probably World War II vintage, but in excellent condition. One day, after driving the Harley to "town," I was walking past a pool hall on King

Street I could have sworn I heard my name called. I stopped and went back to look inside the pool hall and saw two of my high school classmates from Clairton. They had joined the Army together out of high school and were stationed at Schofield Barracks. We had a fun time and they took me to their barracks where we talked about our hometown. Afterwards, whenever I got a hometown newspaper, (my mother sent The Clairton Progress to me regularly throughout my college career) I thumbed my way over to Schofield and visit my old high school friends, Ralph Falk and Franny Furcini, and share news of our hometown. We would have a few beers and I would thumb back to campus.

SWIMMING IN THE DORM

Before heading for Hawaii I had left Provo early to visit family Pittsburgh, as my final exams had been completed. Before I left, on my last night in the dorm, Sandy and I and a few other miscreants decided we would have a swimming party in the dorm. But as it happened, one of the local girls of questionable repute was having a party at her house. The possibility of a tryst with a tawdry trollop trumped the thought of tepid water, so we took the trek to temptation instead. I left early the next day to catch my bus to Pittsburgh. Sandy and the few remaining "scholars" crammed for their remaining final exams.

What I did not know at the time was the evening after I left Sandy and the group, who by that time had completed their final exams, decided to move forward with the dorm swimming party. Of course there was no swimming pool in the dorm, especially not on the second floor where we lived, so we had decided to create one. Most of the dorm residents had gone for the summer and only a few who had late finals were left to implement the plan.

One of the dorm students was an Engineering major and a key member of the plan. He said that to make the swimming pool the metal panel that provided privacy between two toilet stalls in the rest room must first be removed. The panel was just the right size to cover the opening that served as entry into the large rectangle-shaped shower that had four showerheads—one in each corner. The panel was removed from the toilet stalls and the entrance to the shower sealed with dorm towels. The drain cover was removed and the drain was plugged with washcloths and the cover reattached. Then all four showerheads were turned on full force. As the shower began to fill, the weight of the water held the panel in place.

The boys scrambled up to the top of the tile-over-cinderblock shower walls, which did not quite meet the ceiling, and jumped into their pool as it filled. When the shower was perhaps a little more than three-quarters full, a couple of boys jumped in at the same time. The weight of the water and stress on the unreinforced walls was too much to bear and the walls gave way, flooding the shower room, the bathroom, and entire second floor calf deep. The standing water then leaked down onto the first floor, shorting the electrical system in the first floor ceiling. Two of the swimmers, including Sandy, sustained deep gashes on their backs from the jagged cinderblock walls and damaged mortar, as the walls gave way, and they required medical treatment.

Damage to the second floor wing, as well as to the first floor was substantial. The university authorities failed to see any humor in the prank and were, of course, irate. "These miscreants must be punished severely," they all agreed. Every boy who had participated was immediately banned from the dorm, placed on social probation, and their parents assessed the cost of repairs, which of course was substantial. And that is why the Stover Hall dorm was being restored that summer, which allowed me to sneak in and stay for free upon my return from Pittsburgh.

SECOND TERM SOPHOMORE YEAR

I returned to Provo in February 1963 after one fun and fantastic semester in Hawaii. My grade point average from Hawaii was, as we used to say, "Nothing to write home about," unless one was writing bad news. My tennis career was short-lived but the varsity tennis polo shirt was a treasure beyond anything I brought back. I've cherished my memories of that one semester, except for the grades and the tropical skin condition that took an entire semester to eradicate. Had I stayed another semester in Hawaii I would have been placed on academic probation, and without the help of the partial scholarship my funds were evaporating so I decided to return to Provo and do some academic repair work.

Since my original plans had been to stay in Hawaii for an entire school year, I had made no plans for housing upon my early return to the BYU campus. The dorm was out, as it was mid-year and no vacancies existed. It was just as well for by this time I had outgrown the dorm. I wanted some adventure; the type of which off campus housing offered that dormitory life did not.

During my semester at the Church College of Hawaii I kept up correspondence with my friend, Sandy. He told me of the fiasco in the dorm with the shower/swimming pool and said that he was banned for life plus two weeks from ever staying in a BYU dorm. His father had called him from Peru to express his displeasure at the huge bill the university had sent him for Sandy's portion of repairs to the dorm. Sandy said that no phone line was necessary - he was sure he could have heard his father's shouting all the way from Peru to Provo without the aid of a long distance telephone call.

Sandy found a basement apartment in the home of a widow who decided to rent her basement to students in an effort to help with expenses. The landlady, Mrs. Shaw, cleaned the room, did the laundry, and even cooked an occasional weekend meal for no extra charge. She was happy to have the company as well as the rent. There was an extra bed in the basement apartment so when I returned from Hawaii Sandy and I became official roommates. After word had spread of the swimming pool disaster he was unable to find anybody willing to share a dwelling so I gladly accepted. Sandy even volunteered to pick me up at the Salt Lake City airport in one of his several newly acquired cars.

Freedom from the dorm meant a different lifestyle and

that lifestyle meant a need for transportation. Sandy had not owned a car while living in the dorm but during the semester I was in Hawaii he had purchased two or three used "beater" cars (in case one wouldn't start on a cold winter morning). He picked me up at the airport in an old Pontiac and we stayed the weekend at Mrs. Allen's estate before heading to Provo and the next chapter in our lives.

The rest of the semester, Sandy and I attended classes occasionally and drove up to Mrs. Allen's estate nearly every weekend. If BYU served as the basis of my academic education, and the Allphin family served as my extended family, weekends at Mrs. Allen's provided me with cultural experiences few people have the good fortune to enjoy. As I mentioned, she collected homeless animals (she was a major donor and very active in the Salt Lake City ASPCA), and she collected people as well. Most of her menagerie, including a former Soldier of Fortune and outstanding pro golfer, were Libertines.

My fall semester in Hawaii had not done much for my academic progress toward a degree so I took an overload of classes in the spring in an effort to catch up. Nearly all of the general education classes required for graduation are the same, regardless of one's major. Those classes were behind me by this time except for courses in which I had done poorly and needed to repeat. That semester I did surprisingly well catching up and improving my grade point average despite spending so much time at Mrs. Allen's house. My academic repair work continued through the summer as I completed repeated courses and worked in the library. Sister Allphin had promoted me to part time supervisor and that entitled me to a few cents increase in salary as well as more hours.

BOYS AND THEIR TOYS

Part of every boy's life in the 1950s and 60s was a car. Back East, many schools, for lack of parking space, forbade underclassman to drive but at BYU there were no such restrictions. Many a lad and gal loaded up their car and drove to BYU for their freshman year and beyond. On our dorm floor Jim Kimmel had driven his two-tone blue 1956 Chevy from Sacramento, Jon (had the "H" knocked out of him we'd say) Sabourin had a red '48 Chevy with the column gear shift flipped over to the opposite side so he could shift it left handed. Bill Heineke from Salt Lake City drove a 1950 Chevy, John Shaw from Montpelier, Idaho had a red Corvair, and Kermit Hollingshead came from Kansas in his 1957 Ford hardtop that he had named (by painting the name on the side of the car) "Miss Carriage." It was very chic in the 1960s to name one's car with a double entendre.

The car meant freedom and those of us who did not own

one were glad to chip in for gas when we would load up and leave town for a weekend or holiday. Kermit was willing to take a group of lads to Los Angeles for a weekend. We all had a good time – so good in fact that we spent all our money and did not have enough to pay for gas to get home. That fact became evident on the way back to Provo when the engine began to sputter somewhere in Southern Utah, more than a hundred miles from Provo. What to do? We pulled the car to the side of the road and spotted a tractor in a nearby field. All five of us got out of the car and pushed the Ford up next to the tractor. We scouted around until we found a length of hose. Benny the Leech said he had siphoned gas many times in New York and there was nothing to it.

After getting a mouthful of foul tasting liquid, the flow began and we emptied the contents of the tractor tank into Kermit's Ford. Who knew it was diesel? And who knew that diesel was not as a proper fuel to use in a car designed to run on gasoline? Certainly we didn't. The car sputtered and stammered and Kermit was barely able to make it go faster than 15 miles per hour as we limped back into Provo where the car finally died. Another lesson learned.

Sandy discovered his love for cars after he moved from the dorm to Mrs. Shaw's off-campus basement apartment. Neither of us had any mechanical knowledge but during the semester at Mrs. Shaw's house Sandy bought probably a dozen cars at an average cost of $100 to $150 each. We would either shine them up and resell them or drive them until they quit running, then take them to the junkyard and sell them for $25-$30, if all the windows were intact. We decided to take one of the cars, a 1957 Chevy, to Los Angeles to see Kathy, an old girlfriend of Sandy's. They had dated until she dropped out of school but they eventually married and divorced. Kathy's father was a German immigrant who had developed and patented a small part that was used in military rocketry. The government contracts made him a very wealthy man and he moved his family to a beautiful large house on a huge lot on a hill in Van Nuys, in an area of L.A. called "The San Fernando Valley." Kathy's family lived next door to cowboy actor star Chill Wills.

On this particular day we took Sandy's 1957 Chevy and filled the tank with gas. It would take three tanks of gas to get to Los Angeles. Since neither of us had cash for additional gas, and after the fiasco with Kermit's car, we opted for a more sensible solution and took a student who was headed home for the weekend with us. He agreed to pay for gas in exchange for the ride. In the 1960s one could fill the gas tank for $5.00. We left in the late afternoon in order to cross the desert at night and stopped first in Southern Utah then in Las Vegas for gas and to fill up on a 24-hour "All you can eat" buffet meal for 99 cents. Our pit stop in Las Vegas was the Silver Slipper, located on the Strip next door to the Last Frontier and across from the Desert Inn. (Note: The Silver Slipper is gone. The Last Frontier is no more, and the property that housed the Desert Inn now is home to the Wynn). The Silver Slipper Gambling Hall and Saloon had a Mobile gas station in front and was then owned by Bo

Belinsky, the so-called "Bad Boy of Baseball." We had no interest in gambling, only fueling our car and ourselves.

Somewhere outside Riverside, or perhaps it was "San Berdoo" (San Bernardino), the car began to make an awful racket and eventually ground to a halt. It was about 3:00 a.m. and we were in the midst of a barrio. Fortunately Sandy was fluent in Spanish. Unfortunately none of us looked like we belonged in the barrio. We left the car in a parking lot of what appeared to be a car repair shop, noted the name, and hiked toward a nearby freeway onramp. Our passenger found a pay phone and called a family member to come pick him up and Sandy and I stuck our thumbs out on the freeway onramp. Before long a very old truck picked us up and the driver said he was going to the San Fernando Valley. What a stroke of good fortune! The rickety old truck crept along as heavy traffic whizzed by even at that early hour. The old codger asked if we liked dogs and for some reason I took him for a dog hater so I said, "No, I hate them." The truck ground to a halt and he ordered us out on the spot, mumbling something about damn dog haters then he continued down the freeway.

It took us hours to get another ride. A Highway Patrolman chased us off the freeway several times and threatened to give us a ticket if he saw us there again, as he told us "Pedestrians have no business on a freeway." We finally managed to get a few more rides to the general vicinity and about 10:00 a.m. Sandy phoned Kathy who came pick us up.

Since Sandy was comfortable at Kathy's parent's house he decided to stay for a while but I felt I needed to get back to

Provo. He and Kathy took me down to the train station and I spent what little money I had left on a ticket to Delta, Utah, which was as far as my money would take me. That was still about 80 miles shy of Provo but it was all I could afford and I figured I could thumb the rest of the way.

When the train stopped and the conductor bid me adieu, I was expecting a train depot, but instead it was just a wide spot in the track. I thumbed all day without catching a single ride, except for one farmer who took me about a quarter mile then turned off on a dirt road. Finally it began to get dark. I was hungry and when the sun dropped behind the mountains I began to chill, as I had no heavy coat. I was in the middle of nowhere on a highway with very few cars. I had walked and thumbed probably several miles during the day, and I was becoming depressed fast. It must have been 730 or 8:00 p.m. when I walked up to a farmhouse and knocked on the door prepared to beg for a little food or water, but the people inside refused to open the door and threatened me with a shotgun if I didn't leave. I told them I was a BYU student and asked through the closed door if they could call Kathy Jones (the girl I had dated the previous summer and the only phone number I could remember) and I shouted her phone number through the closed door. I asked them to ask her if she would come to pick me up, and that I would wait on the highway. I didn't know if they would call or not but a couple of hours later Kathy and her father pulled up in his old pickup truck. I was shivering from the cold and just sat in a stupor all the way back to Provo. I thanked them profusely when they dropped me off at Mrs. Shaw's basement apartment. Sandy arrived several days later in the repaired '57 Chevy. The rest of the semester I buckled down and studied, waiting for the semester to end.

STEEL MILL SUMMER

The summer after my junior year I returned to Clairton to spend my first full summer there since high school graduation. I was able to land a job as a laborer at Irvin Works, the same steel mill in which my mother worked during the Second World War. She used to tell the story of driving with my father to pick up her pay, which was distributed in cash in a brown envelope. As she opened her pay envelope in the car I was on her lap and my father was driving. It was a hot summer day in pre-air conditioned America and the car windows were all down. My mother pulled a $50 bill from the envelope and waved it in front of my face saying, "This is the biggest bill I'll see for a while. It was no easy task earning this." I reached for the bill, grabbed it, and tossed it out the car window. My father stopped the car and they searched furiously for the $50 bill. But the roadside was overgrown with summer foliage and the green money was difficult to spot among the green plants. Twice they saw it but each time they moved toward the bill, a truck whizzed by and the paper money flew to another resting spot. Finally they were able to retrieve the hard-earned money. As they returned to the car they were both laughing and said, "Can't get mad at the baby. He was playing. We needed to be more careful."

A few weeks later an incident occurred at the mill. Irvin works was a rolling mill; meaning slabs of steel would be rolled into huge coils in an area called "hot strip finish." My mother's job was to mark the six-foot diameter coils with a chalk mark indicating what they were and where they were destined. On a particularly hot, humid August day in the midst of her shift, she passed out while doing her job. She was taken to the infirmary where she apologized to the medical staff, saying that she must not have drunk enough water. The attending physician said, "Perhaps, young lady, but the reason you fainted probably had something to do with the baby boy you're carrying inside you." She was stunned. It was wartime and she needed the job and had not realized she was pregnant. Still she was happy to be having a second son to complete their family – two girls and two boys. They decided to name him George, after her brother who was serving in the Army Air Corps in the South Pacific. But the following April 1945 proved the doctor had erred. The baby was a girl who they named Georgine, but called her by a nickname, Mitzi.

Now, some 20 years after the above episode had occurred I secured a job at the same mill, and traveled the same overgrown road that led to the steel mill. I phoned my old high school buddy, Bob Lees, to tell him I was back for the summer and working at Irvin Works. Bob told me that his uncle, Gibby Lees, was a supervisor at the Irvin Works and might be able to help me get a better paying job than that of laborer so we headed to nearby Elizabeth to meet Uncle Gibby. He was able to finagle the paperwork so that even though I had been hired as a laborer and had the identification number of a laborer, I would be transferred to the Crane Crew as an Electrician's Helper. It was a miserable but very well paying job that convinced me to return to college and finish my degree.

The steel mill was not for me. The Irvin Works, a rolling mill, was huge and hot. Cranes similar to the ones my father had operated as a youth during the Great Depression ran high overhead on tracks, much like railroad tracks, attached to the walls of the building. When one crane went down or became disabled other cranes were affected, as they could not pass the disabled crane.

Andrew Carnegie had the vision of modernizing the steelmaking process. Steel would be made at other mills then delivered in large slabs by barge or rail to rolling mills where the slabs were stored until needed. When orders came in the slabs were scarfed (rust and debris burned off) and pickled (a process of sending the slabs through an acid wash to remove any other impurities that might have hitched a ride during oxidation), as the slabs waited to be rolled. Slabs were next placed in a huge furnace to make them red hot, then positioned on a conveyer under a long line of rollers, progressively providing a smaller and smaller space to pass through. As the slab passed through the rollers, its height became smaller and it lengthened, much like rolling dough to make cookies. Finally what had once been a slab would become a long, thin ribbon of steel. When the hot ribbon, or strip, was the desired length and width, a machine at the end of the rolling line grabbed the tip of the ribbon and spun it into a coil that resembled a car cigarette lighter, only much, much bigger. Coils were marked and cooled, and shipped to auto factories or other clients. The process was called hot strip finish.

As mentioned above, I was hired as a laborer but transferred to a job as an electrician's helper on a crane crew. Huge overhead cranes—dozens of which ran along rails in the mile-long building, manipulated slabs, lifted molten buckets of steel, and doing jobs cranes did. Whenever a crane had a problem (usually as the result of a cable snapping and whipping dangerously) the crane crew was required to get it repaired and back in operation as quickly as possible, as it cost U.S. Steel lots of money to have an idle crane, particularly one that caused others to be idle.

As an incentive, the more quickly crews got the crane back in operation, the more additional monies they were paid. This was called "incentive pay" and if there were lots of breakdowns the crane crew could double or even triple their base pay—which was pretty good to begin with.

The first few nights on the crane crew were an adventure for me; climbing up onto idle cranes for maintenance, replacing and repairing items, and undoing bolts that were bigger in diameter than my thigh. At first I thought that I might drop out of college and do this for a living. That is, until we had the first breakdown of a crane stopped above one of the ovens that heated the steel slabs. The heat was so intense that it burned our hands through the required thick gloves as we climbed the crane to make repairs. We soaked our red handkerchiefs in a water fountain and placed them over our nose and mouth because the air was so hot it would burn our lungs. Once atop the crane, the heat seared through the soles of our regulation steel-tipped work boots. The heat was so intense that the crew was divided into three teams of four; one went up on the crane and worked for several minutes, another stood ready to take its place on the crane, and a third stood on the ground to send necessary tools up in a "nose bag" that took it's name from a horse's feedbag, tethered to a rope. The three teams would rotate and work in mini-shifts until the job was completed and the crane was able to move under its own power. My first experience with a breakdown above a furnace convinced me to return to college and finish my degree. I also lost about ten pounds that night from sweating so profusely

As a safety precaution, whenever a crane broke down, the first duty of the crane crew was to place a red warning light on either side of the disabled crane as a warning to those on either side. Dozens of cranes ran back and forth the length of the mill on tracks that resembled train rails. Electricity ran through the rails and powered the crane, and the crane would complete a circuit by having its metal wheels touch both of the rails. The warning lights were simply red lenses over a heavy-duty light bulb affixed to a 2" X 4" wooden piece of lumber. The lights were on one side of the wood and on the other side were two L-shaped flat metal pieces which, when placed on the rails would complete a circuit and light the bulb. Of course, if a person were to hold onto the L-shaped metal pieces while lowering them onto the rails, that person could become part of the circuit as well and end up fried! A hole at the top of the wood served as the grip, from which to lower the warning light onto the rail. A simple job of hanging a warning light could end in serious injury or death if mishandled. The mill was a very dangerous place to work.

As the summer wore down and my bank account got fatter, my father took me to "Ping" Young, the local Rambler dealer, and I selected a brand new 1963 burgundy colored Rambler American 440H hardtop to drive back to school. The money I earned in the mill paid for most of it and my father chipped in the rest. The car was delivered to me on what was to be my last day working in the mill, a 4:00p.m.-to-midnight shift. That afternoon I drove my first new car to work and parked it in the unpaved parking lot (none of the lots were paved, but they were covered with pebbles or shale rock called "red dog").

My last night on the job began as a slow night with few breakdowns. About 9:30 p.m. the wind began to howl and continued to get stronger. Rain followed, which began coming in at an angle through the huge windows that lined the top of the mill's walls. I did not realize it at the time but the area was about to be hit by a rare (for the Pittsburgh area) tornado.

Somebody yelled, "Close those windows." I was thin and agile and scrambled up like a little monkey to the windows, which were probably 10-15 feet from the floor. As I held onto the windowpane and frame for balance with one hand, I reached out with the other hand for the bar that propped the window open in an effort to pull it shut. At that instant a huge gust of wind hit and I squeezed the windowpane tightly to keep from falling. The impact pushed all four fingers of my gloved hand through the window leaving holes that resembled bullet holes and splintering several of the surrounding glass panes. Fortunately, I was wearing the protective goggles required while working so glass fragments did not injure my eyes, but several shards stuck on the protective leather around the glasses as well as the inside band of my hard hat, shirt, and gloves. I scrambled back down and we rode out the rest of the storm on the floor with our backs against the shuddering wall. It was all over in a few minutes or so, but it was powerful when it hit that it is forever etched in my memory. We learned the next day that several homes, buildings, stores, and a nearby roller rink had been destroyed by the tornado.

After my shift ended my co-workers and I showered and changed clothes. The old vets, who had nicknamed me "Doc" since I was a Psychology major, shook my hand and wished me luck, telling me how lucky I was to get out of this Hell hole, and lecturing me to be sure to finish my education. It was a male bonding moment. When I got to the parking lot I discovered that the swirling tornado had picked up rocks from the parking lot and wrecked every car, including mine! Rocks had swirled through the unpaved lot denting and scratching the body, ruining the paint job, and chipping all the windows of my brand-new car. Fortunately Smokey DeCarlo, the auto body man and neighbor again came to the rescue and replaced all the windows, repainted the car, and had it ready to travel back to Utah in just a couple of days. He even changed the color scheme for me by painting the roof white to simulate a convertible top, and doing a white racing stripe across the body.

On my trip back to Utah, the car was loaded – trunk and top carrier, and three BYU students rode back with me, which paid for my gas and expenses.

SENIOR YEAR

My senior year was the most fun from a curriculum standpoint. I had repeated courses as needed and completed nearly all the required subjects, and saved classes in my major field for my last year. I took several upper division and graduate level Psychology classes that consisted of fieldwork and little classroom drudgery. They included Experimental Psychology that required me to spend lots of time in the lab helping with the experiments, cleaning the rat cages, and so forth. I learned that rats were purchased, and experiments were only done with "naïve" rats, meaning they had not been used in prior experiments. It also meant that when the experiment was over... well, "Goodbye Mr. Rat." The rats were not large and icky like one imagines a sewer rat to be, but small and white and they fit in the palm of one's hand. I would even name some of the rats after my less than favorite professors as well as the president of the university. That made them a little easier to dispose of after the experiments had been completed.

I also took a Psychology class that required me to spend time at the state mental institution located in Provo. The professor cautioned us to always wear our identification badges and told the story of a student who had forgotten his badge but went to a secure part of the hospital anyhow. When he tried to leave he was stopped. He insisted that he was a student volunteer but the orderly said, "Sure you are. Do you know how many times we hear that?" As the story went he spent a week in the hospital before he was discovered. We listened wide-eyed, believing every word, and made mental notes to NEVER enter the hospital without out volunteer ID badge.

Years before my senior year in college, my father had become a devotee of BYU. He did not join the Latter Day Saint (Mormon) religion, but touted it as an excellent one with good moral standards and a strong commitment to education. He touted BYU to anybody who would listen, as a bargain, which one could earn a highly rated private education at a most reasonable cost. Tuition and fees at BYU were comparable to those of state schools in Pennsylvania, the environment was healthy, the culture was clean living, and even his own son, who had been a hopeless dolt as a student in high school, had become a serious student at BYU. My father would have been a wealthy man had he only gone into sales as a career. His sales pitch sent dozens of young Clairton boys to BYU over the years. Two such students who started

BYU during my senior year were Nick Jordan, who was a year ahead of me in high school but had done a stint in the Air Force, and Dennis Zdrale, the son of an immigrant single mother, and who attended the same church as my mother had. I had located a second floor apartment where the three of us would live that year. Nick and Dennis were very serious students and neither was interested in anything Utah or the Mormon religion had to offer aside from a solid education. Hence neither had much of a social life aside from studying. Neither had joined the Mormon Church and both saw this experience as just a means to an end (a college degree from a prestigious private university).

Try as I might, I was unable to get Nick and Dennis to loosen up or become involved in any shenanigans that in my mind typified college life. We rented three upstairs bedrooms in a house that was located on a corner. Each day, as school children passed, a life-size cutout of a child, made of iron and called "Safety Sally," was placed in the middle of the intersection. She was a silhouette four feet high and one inch thick, cut from solid steel, and with a steel base. She was painted to resemble a little girl carrying books. After school hours Safety Sally was rolled to the sidewalk in front of our house. One evening we heard a loud "BANG!" Somebody had forgotten to roll Safety Sally to safety and a car had hit her, knocking the statue to the side, then sped away.

We discussed the irresponsibility of the driver and wondered if that was a quirk or if other drivers would flee the scene if they hit Safety Sally. We walked down to the street and reset Safety Sally in the middle of the intersection then returned to our porch to spy. Soon... BANG! Screech. Another car hit her and sped off. We set her up again and again and again. Each time a different car would hit Sally then speed off. Finally we tired of the prank, left the somewhat bruised Safety Sally on the sidewalk, and returned to our apartment, convinced that drivers in Utah were irresponsible. Nick and Dennis went back to studying and I played a record of a new young singing group called "The Beatles."

A short time later we heard the noise of a police radio coming from a patrol car and saw blinking lights. A police officer knocked on our door and asked if we knew anything about Safety Sally's adventures that night. Dennis and I denied it but Nick, who was so straight it was difficult for him to walk around a corner, spilled the beans. We were given stern lectures, our names taken, and for good measure, were threatened with everything from being sued by the city to doing jail time to being suspended from school for vandalism. Somehow, the blame was placed not on the drivers who had hit Safety Sally and ran but on the ne'er-do-wells who had provided the opportunity. Needless to say, Sally stayed at her assigned position without our interference for the duration of the school year.

"DEAR JOHN"

As mentioned earlier, my father became quite the devotee of Brigham Young University. In his mind the school had changed me from a flake to a scholar and he was not sure what the formula was but he figured that if it worked for me it should work for everybody. My parents had a basement apartment in their home that they rented, and which provided a source of extra income to help defray college expenses for their four kids. Within a year after my departure to the Beehive State, the Mormon missionaries who had been stationed in the area found a home there. Since many missionaries were either Utah natives or BYU alumni, or both, it was one more link between my parents and their son who attended school 2,000 miles from home. My father also admired many of the teachings of the Latter Day Saints, particularly their views and practice regarding family, education, and the word of wisdom, which included abstinence from liquor. Pops kept a bottle of Four Roses on the shelf in his bedroom but rarely took a swig except in the case of a medical necessity or those long winter work shifts that could last 96 consecutive hours or more. He drove the Payloader that loaded City trucks with slag, ashes, and later salt that would clear the City streets and roads during heavy snowfalls and allow for smooth shift changes at the mills that lined the river.

Shortly after the LDS missionaries had moved into the basement apartment in my parent's home, Geno and I purchased the Packard in Utah. One of the missionaries had left a girlfriend behind in Provo and she had sent him a "Dear John," letter. That is code for a breakup letter from the girl who was left behind. My parents phoned me and told me of the young missionary's dilemma and gave me the girl's phone number. I phoned the girl and asked if we could talk. She lived in a rural part of town not far from my dorm so I drove over to pick her up, and we went to a malt shop for soda and to talk about the young lad who I had never met but who was living in the house in which I had grown up. The girl expressed her frustration at being "pinned" (pre-engaged) for two whole years while he served a mission. She did not think it was fair to her or to him, and simply wanted the option to be a free agent. She had nobody in particular that she wanted to date but felt constrained. The situation was just weighing heavily on her. I took the opposing position and reminded her of the commitment her boyfriend had made and that unless she had fallen for another, she might want to reconsider. She agreed and after several hours of conversation we left the malt shop to return her home.

Meanwhile, back in Clairton the young missionary had phoned his girlfriend's house several times only to learn she was not at home but out with another young man (me). There is a two-hour time difference between Clairton and Provo so if I had picked her up at 8:00 p.m. Utah time, it was already 10:00p.m. in the East. By the midnight hour in Clairton it was only 10:00p.m. in Provo and we were on our way back to her house. While we were sipping cider in the malt shop, there had been a pretty good snow and the roads were slick. I'd only recently purchased the Packard and the tires were bald.

As I attempted to follow rural the road back to her house, which had a 90-degree turn, the bald tires went straight and the big Packard dragged a barbed-wire fence partway into a field. The car was stuck and I walked her the rest of the way home. We must have gotten there after 10:30p.m., or 12:30 a.m. in Clairton and her father took me back to my car and helped me get it unstuck. I never spoke to the girl again and often wondered how the poor 19-year old missionary dealt with the thoughts of having lost his girl.

PYRAMID IN PROVO

A second-generation Italian American family who had lived a block up the street from my parents had moved to a more upscale part of the Greater Pittsburgh area. The father had worked his way up to a middle management position in the local steel mill. They had two sons, the older of whom, John, had some challenges. The lad had been in and out of trouble, discharged from the military with an other-than-honorable discharge, and had a few minor scrapes with the law. My father convinced the former neighbor that Brigham Young University was the place to send his son, and thus one more expatriate Clairtonian found himself at Brigham Young University. But John, Jr. viewed Provo from quite a different perspective. The naiveté and trusting culture was just the ticket for John, Jr. to enhance his resume of gaining funding through non-traditional means. He told me about his "revolving checking account." He would open multiple checking accounts then write a check for more money than was in the account. In those pre-computer banking days, the time between a check being written and its processing often took several days, and that time lapse was called the "float." John discovered that he could use money he did not have for several days before the check would be processed, and if at that time he could not cover a check he'd simply write another one on a different account, cash it, and deposit part of the cash in the bank to allow the first check to clear. Although he called the process his "revolving checking account," law enforcement called it check kiting and it was illegal, though rarely prosecuted in those days.

I'm not sure what John spent his money on, whether cars, girls, drugs, gambling, or a combination, but the check amounts that John cashed continued to increase until they became unmanageable, and John would close one account and open another at a different bank. By doing that and changing his residence regularly he was able to juggle his funds for several months. But he needed more money so he took out a loan for 30 days with a finance company. Before the 30 days were up he'd take out a second larger loan to cover the first and give him extra pocket money. Finally the house of cards became so large that he needed a loan of thousands of dollars. One particular finance company was willing to make the loan but required that he get a co-signer given the large amount. John, Jr. told the officials at the finance company that his father was well to do and would co-sign the note. Of course, John, Sr. knew nothing about this and was 2,000 miles away working in a white-collar job in a Pittsburgh area steel mill. But John, Jr. spun a tale to the bank officials that his father was en route to San Francisco on business. As good fortune would have it, he was to change planes in Salt Lake City. John, Jr. would take the contract to his father, have John, Sr. sign it, and return it to the loan company. Trusting souls that they were, they actually gave him the contract and several hours later John, Jr. returned the signed document. Of course, Senior had never been within 2,000 miles of Salt Lake City and Jr. did not even have to leave Provo. He just forged his father's signature and killed some time before returning to pick up his money. By this time John, Jr.'s finances were so convoluted that he was unable to manage his fiscal house of cards and unlike the pyramids of the Middle East, this pyramid scheme came tumbling down around him. John, Jr. was carted off to the hoosegow and several red-faced bank managers wanted his scalp.

One evening my phone rang. It was my father. I could hear sobbing in the background and he told me he was at the home of John, Sr. Junior had been thrown into jail and local officials were getting ready to throw the book at him for charges that ranged from check kiting to forgery. Was there anything I could do? Could I talk to the city attorney and see what needed to be done? John, Sr. wanted his son home and would do anything I suggested. I had full authority to negotiate any type of plea possible that would release his son. Although I was flattered that at the tender age of 20 or so I was asked to do such a major endeavor. I doubted I'd have much success but was certainly willing to try. So I put on my best face and hoped the police department no longer kept files on "the Safety Sally Caper," and headed for the jail.

At the jail I was directed to the courthouse and city attorney's office. Oddly I didn't even consider seeking legal representation for John, Jr. I simply went to see what I could do to help. The City Attorney was an elderly fellow and a BYU grad. The fact that I would soon be a "Y" graduate and fellow alum did not hurt. I explained my father's role in sending dozens of young men to BYU and noted that this was the first and only one who had gone astray. He listened intently and seemed to be impressed. Finally he said, "The State of Utah would just as soon see a bad apple gone." He stated that they would release John, Jr. if the following conditions were met: full restitution for all outstanding monies owed, a fine, a one-way non-transferrable, non-refundable bus ticket to Pittsburgh, a promise that John, Jr. would never return to Utah, and a deputy to accompany a handcuffed John, Jr. as far as the first bus stop in Wyoming or Colorado.

I phoned John, Sr. from the office and outlined the conditions laid out by the City Attorney and he agreed to wire the restitution and fine money (the total was well into the thousands), and he agreed to guarantee any and all other conditions. John, Jr. also agreed, and the next I heard he was back in Pittsburgh. Years later after John, Sr. had passed away, his widow retired to Tucson, Arizona. I visited her once and we had a nice visit talking about old times, but John, Jr. was never mentioned. It was rumored that he had moved to

New Jersey and eventually ended up doing time for other white-collar crimes.

As my final semester at BYU began to wind down I realized that I would soon leave the confines of college and have to go out into the real world of work. I registered at the BYU placement office, checked in regularly, and waited to be called for an interview. The calls were few and far between. It seems that a bachelor's degree in Psychology was not one of the more sought-after degrees in the world of work. There was one interview with an oil company in Cody, Wyoming. Cody is a thousand miles from nowhere and is most famous for having a rodeo and the coldest recorded temperature in the continental United States. I interviewed half-heartedly and was not offered a job. The next interview was with Trane Air Conditioners. Rejected. I even had an interview with J.C. Penney to enter their management-training program. Mr. Penney's first store was in nearby Kemmerer, Wyoming. (What is it with Wyoming?) They told me that they would only consider hiring me if I first shaved off my moustache. Mr. Penney never wore one and employees were required to be clean-shaven. I scratched them off my list and kept my moustache. There just were not a lot of job offers for a Psychology bachelor degree holder. Most Psych graduates went to grad school. I was tired of school and had neither the will nor the funds to continue, nor the grades to get into a top level graduate school.

Sometime during the final semester of my senior year, 1964, my best friend, roommate, and occasional partner in shady behavior, Sandy, told me that Mrs. Allen had called and invited us to one of her Sunday parties—as GUESTS! She said that she was having "some of the soldiers over," and thought we might enjoy meeting them. I did not know who the soldiers were but knew she was active in nearly every charitable cause and assumed they might have included a few enlisted men about our age from one of the nearby military bases. I was both flattered and honored that she now saw us as "men" worthy of being invited to one of her parties. I put on my Sunday best so as not to embarrass her, or us, and Sandy and I headed up to Salt Lake City. Sandy was not the least bit nervous as this seemed to be a matter-of-fact event for him. He reeked of social graces, knew of world politics, and was fluent in three languages. I on the other hand, felt like a country bumpkin going to his first formal dance.

We arrived early in the afternoon and the chauffer, "Joey," took our car. The place looked so grand! We used the front entrance instead of our usual back area where our weekend apartment was located. Mrs. Allen, dressed to the nines with what looked like 50 pounds of jewelry, was a gracious hostess and as soon as she saw us she said, "Oh, do come and meet the soldiers," and proceeded to introduce us to two Generals, one Admiral, and a couple of Colonels. As it turned out, this was a special party being given in honor of Mrs. Allen's cousin, General Richard I. Krone, of the U.S. Army Medical Corps. He had just been promoted from the staff at Walter Reed Hospital to head Madigan General Hospital in Washington state, as well as being given another star. Sandy pulled me aside and whispered that I was to call her Didi as did all her other guests. That way neither of us would be embarrassed. It was awesome talking to the "soldiers" and I soon found myself alone in conversation with General Krone.

"I understand you are about to graduate with a psychology degree," said the General.

"Yes, sir."

"Have you given any thought to your military service?"

"Some, but nothing definite."

"My cousin thinks highly of you. Would you consider the Army Medical Corps?" I was too stunned to answer so he continued; "You would come into the Army with a direct commission as either a First Lieutenant or a Captain, as a psychologist. Your base of training would be Fort Sam Houston and if you don't golf, you will certainly learn while there." He continued, "The Army will pay for any advanced training or degrees that are required. Give it some thought. It will keep you off the battlefield."

I shook his hand and thanked him, and that night drove back to Provo in a trance. There have been some momentous, life changing experiences in my lifetime; ending up at BYU when I never thought I would get into college; developing writing skills that would help me publish, a chance meeting with my roomie, and so on. Other decisions were momentous as well but on the other end of the continuum and probably not the ones I should have made. Such was the decision to not go into the Army Medical Corps with a Direct Commission. My father discouraged it saying all the officers in the military were drunks. Several of my classmates, including Sandy, cautioned me that fighting was heating up in Viet Nam and it would be a brutal place to serve. It was a huge decision but in the end my sin was one of omission rather than one of commission. I simply did not pursue the offer to become a commissioned officer, and neither did General Krone pursue me after that one conversation. Who knows how my life might have been different had I taken him up on his offer?

LOVES AND LOVERS

I had not dated anyone seriously for any extended period of time throughout my college career. I had a crush on Betsy, my high school chum who introduced me to BYU. She was gorgeous, at least to me. She was 5'9" with blond hair, blue eyes, and milky skin. She was smart, came from a terrific family and was in excellent physical condition. She jogged long before it was fashionable. But she was so perfect in my young eyes that I was too intimidated to even consider anything beyond a Platonic friendship. Then, after one semester, she was gone. There was Margie, the nurse from England whose father sold Nuclear Fallout shelters, and whose best friend Vickie became Geno's wife. Margie and I had a young, intense, highly erotic relationship, my first and hers as well. There were others, just as any college lad would have had. Margie was the most passionate, but like any flame that burns brightly, it eventually flickers. Margie and I drifted apart after that. She had the heart of a hippie. She was very creative, smart, and loved to play just outside the rules. We had tons of fun together but were mostly playthings to one another. Margie eventually married Sid and had three or four kids before the hippie part of her personality overtook her. One day she just left her family and moved to a commune. Sid rarely heard from her after that.

Kathy Jones was the blonde, blue-eyed girl from Orem who had a 1956 Rambler. We dated for a while but were really more buddies than lovers. She seemed so straight and naïve. She fed me one summer at the movie theater where she worked and had free food as a perk, and she and her father came to pick me up after Sandy's car broke down and my subsequent train ride from California. Years later when we were both married. I ran into her and her husband at a club in Salt Lake City. Kathy did not seem to be happy.

It was the culture at BYU to identify a mate "for time and all eternity," and I just didn't see myself as part of that equation. Perhaps it was partly my youthful rebellion, but eternity seemed like such a long time!

There were several other dates during my college life, mostly casual. I simply have always been unable to take seriously traditional rules and by extension while at BYU, those of the Mormon or any other religion. As part of convincing myself that I was still an individual on what I sometimes considered to be a campus of sheep, I listened to radio music that was sort of edgy at the time. One such musical format came from an FM radio station that played mostly jazz. Somehow I got to know the disc Jockey that did call-in requests late at night. We became friends and I often hung out at the station on weekends, taking calls mostly from women who requested particular songs. John the DJ would whisper into the mike when he talked and in those days that was not only considered very sexy, but right on the edge of announcing oneself as a bad boy. We came up with a show called "Rap Around." Rap was not a music genre but a hip word for "talk." Mostly female callers would phone in requests and talk on the air for a few minutes until another caller would ring. Then John would switch "caller number one" to me off the air and I'd continue the conversation off air.

We would often talk to the female callers as the music played and on one occasion a regular started to call the station whenever she knew I was there. I asked her out and we started to date. She was also a senior at BYU with the odd name of Sherma Newbold. She would eventually become my first wife.

COLLEGE IS OVER,
LIFE BEGINS

By April of my senior year I was getting desperate, as I had no solid job prospects. I was a Psychology major with a bachelor degree and no desire for the pursuit of an advanced degree. That combination qualified me to sell cars, which I did, or enter some sort of management training program. All three of my sisters had attended (then) Millersville State Teachers College in Pennsylvania, a few hundred miles from Clairton and in Amish country. My eldest sister, Maryann, became a librarian. The youngest, Mitzi, became a teacher. Kathy, the middle sister married after one year of college. She and her husband went into the restaurant business.

When my eldest sister, Mary Ann, left for college my parents took her to Millersville State Teachers College for orientation and to get settled. My father befriended a young professor. They became close friends and remained so for decades as the young professor became a department chair, administrator, and eventually became the president of the college. It was that connection that proved fortuitous while I was looking for a job prior to my graduation. As I was striking out at every interview in Utah, my father called this family friend who in turn phoned another longtime friend of his, a superintendent of a small rural school district in southeastern Pennsylvania. One evening I received a phone call from the superintendent. He made small talk for a while and I was trying to figure out why he was calling. Finally, he popped the question; would I consider coming back to Pennsylvania to accept a teaching position? I was a little taken aback, but gathered myself and explained that I was a Psychology major and not an Education major. He asked how my job search was going with my Bachelor of Science degree in Psychology. I had to admit he had me there.

He continued in his recruitment mode, "There is an acute shortage of teachers these days, particularly in rural areas. If you would go to the Millersville College this summer and pick up a couple of education classes to show you are working toward a teaching certificate, I'm sure I could get the state to issue you an emergency teaching certificate that would be provisional and allow you to teach."

I thought for a moment and said, "I don't know how to teach."

He had a ready response, "I assume you went to school for 12 years before attending college for the past four. Am I right?"

"Yes," I answered slowly and suspiciously.

"Well then, you've been observing teaching practices for the past 16 years. Certainly you know SOMETHING about what makes a good teacher." He had me there too.

"What would I teach?"

By now I could almost hear sarcasm in his voice, "Hmmm, let's see, after 16 years of education I would assume you have mastered at least the sixth grade curriculum. We will put you in a brand new school that contains grades six, seven, and eight. There will be five other sixth grade teachers to help you. What do you say?" I paused, processing what he said when he added, and "Oh... and you will be getting full pay. The state minimum is $4,500 per year but our district will start you at $4,800." I agreed. I figured I would teach for a year until I decided what I wanted to do when I grew up. I discovered later that the Oxford Middle School, to which I had been assigned, was Pennsylvania's first middle school. The superintendent had gotten the State to approve my "emergency teaching certificate" by using the logic that a Psychology major would be a good fit in the experiment that was to be called a middle school.

Meanwhile, back in Provo, Sherma and I had dated perhaps a dozen times over the final semester of our senior year. She was different from any girl I had dated at BYU; not what I would call "churchy," but certainly not rebellious. She fit the Brigham Young University coed profile; blond hair and blue eyes and Danish/English heritage. Before we began dating she had gone out a couple of times with a BYU foreign student from Persia. Persia was code for Iran. For some reason many wealthy non-Mormon Iranians attended BYU. He had proposed to her on the second date telling her she would live in wealth and be the number one wife. I'm not sure what frightened her more, leaving the safety of Utah or marrying a wealthy Persian who had plans for multiple wives, but she clearly was in the midst of trying to end the relationship when I happened on the scene and I helped her do that.

On our second or third date her parents drove down (as they did nearly every weekend) from the Salt Lake City area and took her to dinner. She invited me to join them, which I did. It was a most interesting night. Her father Bill drove the big white Chevy station wagon that doubled as a delivery vehicle for her mother Dorthea's flower shop, but it was clear that Dorthea was in charge. She was loud and rough around the edges and apparently it made no difference that I was in the car with her daughter. Dorthea screamed at Bill regardless of what he did. He drove too fast or too slow, ran the stoplight or waited too long. She reminded me of Calamity Jane but without the singing voice or personality. She was in charge regardless of the circumstance. She was opinionated and shared her point of view with everybody, from the waiter at the restaurant to the owner. I had never seen anyone quite like her. I should have taken that as a cue and eased out of the relationship but instead felt I that I needed to protect the young damsel from the overbearing mother.

Dorthea was not shy about letting the entire world know

she was in charge. She quickly told me that she was not prepared to let any man boss her. She had been unhappy with the salary her husband made so she kept chickens at the house and earned extra cash selling eggs until her children flew the coop. Next, she got a job at the Salt Lake City newspaper. When one of her male bosses reprimanded her she quit, took out a loan and purchased a flower shop, which she had turned into a thriving business. Bill and Dorothea had one son who lived in California with his 12 children, and then 10 years later they had a daughter. That was to have been their entire family but eight years after the daughter's birth Dorthea had a menopause surprise baby, Sherma, who was practically an only child as her sister was 8 years her senior and her brother 18 years her senior.

We dated for the rest of the semester and when it came time for me to leave for Pennsylvania she said, "I know I'll never see you again."

In my best "It'll be alright, Little Lady" impression of John Wayne I said, "What you mean? I'll come back after my year in Pennsylvania and we'll be married." I'm not sure where that came from as we had been dating exclusively but had not even discussed marriage. But I had made a commitment of sorts and perhaps I figured "out of sight out of mind," but in reality, probably did not think much about it at all.

When she announced to her parents that we planned to marry in a year, Dorthea seemed to take it in stride. She promised Sherma a choice building lot located near the house she and Bill owned. It was to be a pre-engagement gift. Her father had given the lot to her. The lot was on the edge of 30 or so acres that Sherma's parents owned and it had a beautiful view of the valley. She also promised Sherma a car if she came to work in the flower shop and learned the flower business instead of staying in Provo to finish her degree. Dorthea talked a good game—she made plenty of promises but too often did not deliver. There was no gift of a building lot, and no car. I left to teach school in Pennsylvania, and Sherma did not return to BYU finish her last three courses for her Sociology degree, but instead moved in with her mother and began to manage the flower shop.

By the time Sherma was planning to return to Salt Lake City at the end of the semester to work in the flower shops, her mother had not yet purchased a car. She had been driving the shop's delivery van but had no transportation of her own. I scouted the area for a good used car and found a 10-year old green Pontiac with just less than 100,000 miles. It seemed to run well and the price was right—about $300 as I recall. The car lot owner allowed me to put half down and pay the balance in monthly installments, which I agreed to send from Pennsylvania. It turned out to be an excellent purchase, as that winter was an especially cold one in Utah and the Pontiac was the only car at her parent's house that started every morning. With Sherma living at home with her parents and in possession of a job as a florist and a car, I left to cross the country for my first real job as a college graduate.

For the previous four years as a college kid I had shucked and jived and flimmed and flammed and worked in the library, and did all manner of entrepreneurial activities to help pay my way through college. My parents, of course, bore much of the financial burden but I was very sensitive that three other family members were in college and tried my best to assume some of the financial burden. Those were all "catch-as-catch-can" jobs. To have a real job with real responsibilities in the real world is something I had not been trained for or considered. Since I graduated debt free I would have more money than I had ever had in my life, without any school-related fiscal obligations. Although I was about to graduate debt-free I would soon find myself deep within the web of financial morass.

The day before the call came from the Superintendent in Pennsylvania I had been out window-shopping cars. Ford had just released a new sports car called the Mustang. It cost around $2,000. A new Cadillac cost about $5,500. I figured if I would be earning almost as much as the price of a new Cadillac, that must be pretty good money. Using that logic, and having no other offers, I accepted the teaching job.

The summer flew by. I took a couple of basic courses at the Millersville State Teachers College, the school all three of my sisters had attended, located near Oxford. In early September I began my first real job as a sixth grade teacher in the Oxford Area School District. I usually joke that my first job out of college was a teaching position at Oxford.

FROM COLLEGE KID TO ADULTHOOD

It was 1964 and there was an acute shortage of teachers, especially males, and especially in the elementary grades. The superintendent had told me that as a male teaching elementary grades I would always be a desired commodity. I walked into my classroom in a brand new school as the accidental teacher. There I was again, a stranger in a strange land. A teacher who had never even student taught and who had just two summer school teacher education classes under his belt. I was no more prepared to teach than I was to be a college lad four years earlier, but I had managed to muddle through that component of wacademia and was confident I could get by in this new venture.

The sixth grade classes at Oxford Area Middle School were self contained (one teacher taught all subjects) and homogeneously grouped, (the entirety of grade six students was divided by academic ability). I was assigned to teach the fifth (next to the bottom) of six groups. With absolutely no teacher training and no student teaching, (I don't even remember having any curriculum guides), I was given teacher's edition textbooks and my responsibility was to teach sixth grade English, Math, History, Geography, Music, Art, and whatever else was on the schedule. The core courses could be taught by planning one day ahead of the students but art? I had no sense of art. Music? I couldn't even play the radio on key! But there is no confidence like that of a young fool and I had plenty of confidence. The principal, E. Worth Brown, had not had a say in selecting me but was supportive.

To make matters even more interesting, a few miles up the road was the small predominantly Black college, Lincoln University. In 1964 the Peace Corps was a volunteer agency in full swing. A group of Peace Corps volunteers was being trained at Lincoln University to teach school in the newly minted country of Tanzania (Tanganyika and Zanzibar had merged to form the new country). Part of the Peace Corps volunteers training included student teaching for all who were to teach school in Tanzania. Since our small rural school district encompassed Lincoln University, every teacher in the district, including myself, was assigned a student teacher. Picture this; I had neither student-teacher training nor teaching experience and knew precious little about teaching, yet within a few weeks of my initial school teaching experience I was to become Master Teacher to a student teacher. Her name was Phyllis Disney, she was from

Denver, supposedly was the niece of Walt Disney, and had already taken student teaching twice in Denver. She actually had more teaching experience than I did yet I was the Master Teacher! Somehow we muddled through together.

By mid-November the Peace Corps student teachers had completed their training with us and were on their way to Africa. The balance of the semester was exhausting and a real challenge as I was alone in the classroom with 30 sixth graders who had scored next to the bottom academically. But I gave it everything I had. The work was so exhausting that I would often stop on the way home and pick up a hoagie (since it had all the elements of good nutrition - meat, veggies, bread, etc.), take it home, eat it, and by 4:30 p.m. go to bed and sleep through until the next morning.

I don't think I damaged the kids too much. In fact, there were some advantages to my lack of preparation. Since I had not been trained as a "standardized test" teacher, I did a lot of individual instruction, tutored after school, visited homes of students, and really became involved in the community. One little African American girl, Chloe, was the daughter of itinerant mushroom pickers (Oxford, Pennsylvania was a big mushroom producing area). I had never seen abject poverty before going into her home. I worked with Chloe, who had not attended school much because her parents followed the picking seasons up and down the Eastern Seaboard. But she really made progress during that year and her parents would send me a peck of mushrooms each week as a thank you. I never before had eaten mushrooms but after that year they became a favorite.

Because I was reared the only boy with three sisters my only chores at home had been to take out the garbage. In college I did my own laundry but had all wash-and-wear clothes so I did no ironing. During those college years I either lived in the dorm or a basement apartment, where Mrs. Shaw, the landlady, did all the cleaning, laundry, and most of the cooking. Thus at age 21 I was not only ill prepared for the teaching profession but also for bachelorhood and living on my own. I ate out regularly or brought take-out food home, and on weekends, usually drove the 300 miles to my parents' home where my mother did my laundry, cooked, and sent me back with prepared meals.

One day I decided to stretch my bachelor abilities and bought a package of "Heat-Em-And-Eat-Em" cinnamon rolls for the following morning's breakfast. I rarely ate breakfast but this was going to be the new me. I woke up early, put the package in the oven, turned up the oven to 300 degrees, or whatever it said on the directions. I then showered, dressed, and went to school. When I returned home that night the apartment stank of burned stuff and there were six cinders in the oven—still baking at 300 degrees. Fortunately the apartment did not catch fire. I did not make a very good bachelor.

DATING AND ANOTHER BRUSH WITH THE MILITARY

The $4800 annual salary that sounded like such a huge amount of money during my conversation with the super-intendent turned out to be not quite the financial bonanza I had anticipated. After all deductions my monthly salary was about $325. I had never had regular income before and went wild that year. First thing I did was to get rid of my year-old '63 Rambler American that I had gotten the previous sum-mer with money saved up by working in the steel mill. I'd managed to put nearly 40,000 miles on the Rambler in less than a year by driving coast-to-coast and border-to-border. I traded it for a brand new, top of the line 1964 Buick Electra 225 convertible. Monthly car payments were $107.37. Rent was another $75 and since I ate all my meals out it did not take long to use up $325 in monthly salary before I paid my phone, utilities, gasoline, trips to Pittsburgh every other week, and other expenses. By the end of my first year teaching I had gone from being debt free to being more than $10,000 in debt—more than double my annual salary!

I did not think anything would become of my proposed marriage to Sherma, so on my visits to my parent's home I dated. One gal was a stewardess named Judy. She lived in nearby Finleyville, a rural community. She had a best friend named Loraine and Judy and I and Loraine and my buddy Jay began to double date. Jay had recently completed his military obligation and returned to work in the local steel mill. Our first double date was a drive-in movie and Jay, sitting in the back seat, had forgotten Loraine's name. We went to the snack bar for popcorn (Jay and I) and he told me he'd forgotten her name. I said I couldn't remember it either but I would figure out a way to tell him, so when we returned, I whispered to Judy, "I forgot your friend's name." She said it was Loraine, and I shouted "LO-RAIN!" She said, "What?" and I asked if she wanted some popcorn. She said no and Jay chuckled. Jay and Lorain became and item and were married and enjoy wedded bliss to this day. My two best friends were Geno and Jay and I got them both married off under similar circumstances.

I casually suggested that Judy come to visit me sometime, and sure enough one Friday my phone rang and she said she was at the Baltimore airport waiting for me. By this time (spring 1965), unable to keep up the payments, I had sold the Buick and bought a '64 Rambler convertible with a "twin stick" shift. One stick was to change gears and the other was to place the transmission in or out of overdrive (an extra gear for better gas mileage at highway speeds). A white button on the top of the overdrive stick would take the car out of overdrive and provide a passing gear or burst of speed as needed. It was a unique transmission setup and Rambler only made it that year. I've never seen another one like it.

Baltimore was only 45 minutes away so I drove down to pick Judy up for a weekend Oxford. She was gorgeous but a bit naive. She saw my briefcase that had been embossed with my initials (ARN) and asked me what ARN stood for. I said, tongue-in-cheek that I'm really not a teacher, that's just my cover. I'm actually a spy and ARN is my code name. She said, "REALLY?" She asked me about the white button on top of the overdrive stick and I said, "Well, since I'm a spy, this car was built with an ejection button. If I push it you will be ejected." She said, "Wow!"

Before the weekend was over I had spun a tale worthy of a James Bond movie script about the Russians being after me, that a complete secret background check was done on her before I was allowed to date her, and if she ever doesn't hear from me, she should go to the FBI and report me missing. I'm sure I told her other ridiculous stuff that I can't remember, and after that weekend I lost interest in her. I had higher priorities than dating. My bills were piling up. In an effort to get out of the financial straits, I had my gas turned off, stopped driving to Pittsburgh on weekends, and even had my phone disconnected, as my college friends were all over the country and my phone bills were higher than my rent.

Several weeks after the Judy caper, while on my way to school I stopped by the post office where I received my mail in a box. I discovered a card in the box that indicated I had a registered letter awaiting me. I said to myself, "Oh, no. Here I am 21 years old, Draft Status 1-A, and this has to be my draft notice! If I have to go to Viet Nam I want to fly, not march." So I called in to the school and requested a substitute for my classes, took a sick day, and headed for Willow Grove Naval Air Station, about 50 miles away, to see if I could get into Naval Aviation. It was a Monday morning and as luck would have it, when I arrived there were 11 men preparing to take the entrance exams. They simply added me as the 12th applicant to replace somebody who had not shown up.

The tests seemed easy. I had been in the BYU ROTC program for one year but one of the student officers told me I was not officer material and that I should drop out of ROTC, which I did. But before doing so I was able to take the test for pilot training. Oddly enough (to me anyhow) I had scored high enough on the test to be a navigator, but not high enough to be a pilot. Now, four years or so later I was taking a similar test that seemed to be much easier than it had been when I had taken it as a freshman. Besides the exams, which lasted most of the day, we were billeted in the BOQ (Bachelor Officer's Quarters) and each applicant was taken for a ride in a T-33 aircraft – a training jet used in teaching new pilot trainees. It was a two-day blast and I seriously thought I might enjoy my time during the Viet Nam war flying over the poor grunts on the ground.

After two days of mental and physical tests only three of us had passed everything required for pilot training. We three were told we had one more interview (with a psychiatrist!) and then we were to return home while they ran our background checks, and within 4-6 weeks we would hear from the Navy. Once the background checks had cleared they would tell us where and when to report—most likely Pensacola, Florida. By this time I had not told anyone at the Naval Station about the draft notice sitting in my post office box in Oxford so I felt I needed level with the shrink. I told him that I had a very strong feeling I was going to be drafted. He picked up his pencil and pad and said, "Oh really? How long have you been having these feelings?"

I said, "No, no, you don't understand." Then I proceeded to tell him that I had just gotten a registered letter, my draft notice I presume, that Monday morning. I told him I had not retrieved the letter so technically I had not been notified, but the letter was waiting for me at my post office. He said he'd call my draft board, have me reclassified as active reserve, and the draft notice would be voided.

I was so pumped driving home! I had beaten the system and would live every boy's dream—to fly! I gave no thought to the possible danger of flying bombing runs over Viet Nam, landing on an aircraft carrier, or anything of that ilk. Instead I just wallowed in the romance of it all, picturing myself first as an Officer and a Gentleman, military pilot, then with a career as a commercial pilot with the airlines.

I returned to Oxford and went directly to my mailbox,

pulled out the registered letter notification, and went to the desk to retrieve the registered letter that was from...JUDY! She had not heard from me, my phone had been disconnected, and she did not want to go to the FBI to report me missing until she tried the registered letter. I laughed; then it hit me... MY GOD! WHAT HAD I DONE?????????? Planes get shot down over Viet Nam and pilots are taken prisoner! Look what happened to John McCain!

The father of one of my students was a lawyer so I went straight to him for counsel, and remember saying to him, "Will you quit laughing and tell me what to do???"

He told me not to worry, that officially I could not sign up until the Navy did the background check, a process that protects both the Navy and gives the applicant a "cooling off period." He said to just ignore their letters, as I had not made a legal commitment.

By virtue of the fact that I was classified1-A, and since I told the psychiatrist that I thought my draft notice was awaiting me, the draft board changed my classification on the spot to 2-Y or something like that. I'm not exactly sure what that designation meant but I used to tell people that it meant I'd be called up after women and children.

The Christmas holidays were juxtaposition from my college days to my first year teaching. Instead of visiting my parents as I had done as a student, I returned to Utah to see what was happening on that front. Yes, I had sort of become engaged but not really, at least not in my mind. I'm not sure what my intent was when I visited Utah—to release her from the engagement or to firm it up. When I landed in Salt Lake City I rented a Mustang and went to see Sherma. Her mother was busily planning her daughter's June wedding and so I just went along with the program. We were both so immature; neither of us realized the responsibilities of marriage.

THE ACCIDENTAL HUSBAND

In June of 1965, after I completed my first year of teaching, I left Pennsylvania and returned to Utah and to be married. We were both so young, but the law said we were adults. Perhaps I thought it would show my father that I was mature. Perhaps it was to show the world that I would live up to my word. It might have been because my personality is that of a rescuer and fixer and she seemed to need rescued from a tyrannical mother. But most likely it was because neither of us had a confrontational personality so we married by default. Sherma had left BYU less than one semester short of a degree in Sociology and went to work for her mother. Dorothea soon purchased a second flower shop and named it Cherlynn's, a play on her two daughter's names—Sherma and Marilyn. We married in June 1965, and other than my parents and sister, the bride was about the only person I knew at the wedding and I didn't know her very well.

I spent the summer looking for a job. I sold cars for a week or so until the dealership determined I was not cut out for that line of work. If a customer asked what was wrong with a used car, I would tell him. My career as a car salesman was short lived. I delivered flowers for the flower shops and tried for several other jobs but that Bachelor's degree in Psychology was not helping much. The superintendent in Oxford had told me that as a male teaching in elementary school, I would always have a job, and that was the case everywhere except in Utah. There the boys went on missions and returned to marry the girls who got teaching degrees to put their men through the rest of their college. No teaching jobs were available for me in Utah.

Sherma was from South Jordan, south of Salt Lake City. Her family had come across the plains with Brigham Young in 1847. It seemed she was related to just about everybody between Provo and Ogden. That fact did not help me find long-term gainful employment. Although her uncle was superintendent of the largest school district in the area, no teaching job was forthcoming for me in large part because I had no teaching credential and only one year of teaching experience. As the summer came to a close, we had been married just over a month and were living in a small, second story apartment that her mother had located for us. The apartment was situated around the corner from the flower shop and a block from Cottonwood Hospital. It was bad enough having to listen to ambulance sirens at all hours of the night but our telephone number was just one digit off from the hospital emergency number. Talk about sleepless nights! To add to the frustration Dorthea would phone every morning at 6:00 a.m. for no other reason than to talk to her little girl. It was maddening but would get worse. Dorthea would start a fight with Sherma on the phone and Sherma would become so upset she'd slam the phone onto the receiver. Not the best way to start a day. Soon her mother and I became enemies. She accused me of trying to steal her business. When she went on a rant everybody in the immediate vicinity would back down. I would not. That made me her public enemy #1.

I really needed to find a job that would pay for food, clothing, and shelter and retire some of the massive debt I accrued during my year as a bachelor. Although Sherma was officially the manager of the second flower shop, Dorthea treated her like any other employee and paid her minimally on the books and sporadic monies off the books.

After a summer of unsuccessful job seeking attempts, by August I bid my young bride adieu, got in my car, and began to drive, stellar teacher evaluations in hand. My plan was drive north to the Canadian border, west to the Pacific Ocean, south to the Mexican border, and east to Tucson then back up to Salt Lake City. During the drive I would stop at every little village and town and offer my services as a male elementary schoolteacher.

As I drove north past Ogden, Utah I made stops at several towns including Tremonton, Utah and Downey, Idaho. All had their quotas filled for the upcoming year so I continued onward. By noon I pulled into Pocatello, Idaho and walked into the administrative offices of Idaho School District #25. Everybody was out to lunch except one assistant superintendent who was eating at his desk. I no sooner told him that I was a male (which he could no doubt tell by looking at me), with elementary teaching experience than he said, "Don't leave this room!" as he scurried around to find a contract. I signed it on the spot and was assigned to teach the sixth grade at Tendoy Elementary School for the next two years. The state granted me a two-year provisional teaching certificate during which time I picked up the courses I needed at Idaho State University to become a licensed teacher. Still I had no student teaching experience but the money was getting a little better. I had been making $4,800 a year in Pennsylvania but was earning a whopping annual salary of $5,300 in Idaho.

The plan was to teach during the week and return to Salt Lake City and married life on weekends. That worked for a few weekends but soon, each time I got ready to return to Pocatello, Sherma would cry and say, "I miss you. I can't stand living like this." Once again my young male hero ego shifted into the "fix-it" mode. I told her I would find a house to rent in Pocatello and we would set up our home in Idaho. She agreed and said she would let her mother know. A few weeks later I arrived from Pocatello in a rented truck, loaded the contents of our apartment, and off we went to a cute little one-bedroom bungalow, caddy-corner (although in Idaho and Utah they say "kitty-corner") to Washington Elementary School.

My efforts to reduce my debt took many forms including spending frugally for the household, working multiple jobs, finding my wife a job, and cutting corners wherever I was able. One such corner had to do with licensing my car. The Rambler convertible I had purchased in Pennsylvania was still my primary vehicle. It also still had Pennsylvania license plates, which by that time had expired. My logic was that since there were not many Pennsylvania license plates in Idaho, and since it was very difficult to tell the plates were expired without looking at the actual registration, I would take a chance on not registering the car in Idaho and driving on my expired Pennsylvania tags. That worked for the two years I was in Idaho. I was never stopped, but I was nearly caught one day because my students were working on a project. They needed some supplies and the principal gave me cash to go to a store in downtown Pocatello to purchase the supplies. I took a couple of kids with me who knew exactly what was needed. The main street in downtown Pocatello was a one-way street with several lanes of traffic. I saw a parking space in front of the store that had the items we needed so I crossed two lanes to get to it—without looking in my blind spot. My car struck the car next to me and although the damage was minimal (the chrome circle around her headlight was scratched) the car owner insisted we call the police. I sent the kids inside the store and waited, trying to think of how to explain my expired tags. When the officer arrived he had us exchange information and asked for my registration. When I retrieved it I tried to look shocked and said, "Can you believe it? I go to Salt Lake each weekend and my son was playing in the car. He must have taken the current registration. All I have is this expired one."

I held my breath and the officer said, "I understand. I have four kids myself (I did not have any except my imaginary son in the story I just told). "I can just imagine my little tyke doing something like that."

He did not write me up and the kids came out of the store with the items they needed. I found a replacement in a junkyard for the damaged part on the car I had hit and it cost less than $5.00. The gods were smiling on me that day. What could have been a tragedy due to my penny-pinching and inattentive driving turned out to be just a scare. I continued with the expired tags with no further incidents but became a much more cautious driver.

DAYTIME, NIGHTTIME IN POCATELLO

A h, the things a young body is able to tolerate. In my youth I was able to get by with a minimum amount of sleep. I was also about $10,000 in debt as the result of poor fiscal management during my year as a bachelor in Pennsylvania. Thus my early years of marriage consisted in large part of efforts to extricate myself from debt. In my mind, that goal would be most easily achieved by increasing the family income. To that end, we found my wife a job in the Admissions and Records office at Idaho State University. In addition to my teaching the sixth grade I tutored math privately after school and took a job working the night shift at a Richfield gas station just off the Interstate 15. My typical day would be to teach from 8-3, then tutor for an hour or so, take a nap, have dinner, and then work at the service station from 10:00 p.m. until 6:00 a.m. take a shower, have some breakfast, and be at school by eight.

My day was designed around being frugal. At school I ate school lunches or something brought from home. When an extremely wet fall prohibited equipment into the potato fields, rather than let them rot, the fields were opened up to the public. Anything one could pick and carry, one could have for free. We ate lots and lots of potatoes that winter.

Nights were spent in the gas station. The gas pumps were mechanical, not digital or computer activated. Hence, after gas was pumped and the hose returned to the pump, a small residual quantity of gasoline remained in the hose. After each sale I would "drain the hose" into a gas can that I kept next to the pumps and when the shift was over I usually had a gallon or two of free gas in the can to add to my own car's gas tank.

I discovered that I was not the only Clairton alum who had traveled. One night about 3:00 a.m. a silver Volkswagen with Montana license plates pulled off the freeway and up to the pump. The driver said, "Fill 'er up," and got out of the car to stretch. As I looked at him I was stunned. It was Bob Potts, a high school classmate. He had been living in Montana and was moving to the Bay area of Northern California and would later hook up with Geno Tolari whose career had taken him to Silicon Valley. Small world. I asked Bob how he happened to be in Montana and what he hoped to do in San Francisco that could not be done in Montana. Bob told me that Montana was cold as a witch's.... well, it was really cold! Geno, who had become very successful in the Silicon Valley, had helped most of Bob's family move from Clairton to that area. Bob was the eldest child and hoped to find work and be closer to his family. I filled his gas tank, bid him adieu, and wished him the best. I later learned that Bob had found work and spent quality time with his family before passing away a few years ago.

One benefit to working nights at the gas station is the time between customers. Aside from the occasional flat tire, people rarely came in to have cars serviced late at night and there was plenty of free time between gas fill-ups and oil changes. Never one to be idle, I decided to use that time to try to become a writer. Aspiring writers had a sequence of steps to conquer in order to build a resume. The first was "pulp" magazines, or those that printed fiction stories mostly about "true" romance. Their target audience was teen and pre-teen girls. Once an author published in the pulps s/he could continue to do so, or move onto paperback novels, or even the so-called slicks, magazines such as Look, Life, or other upscale magazines. I decided to start with the pulps.

I further decided to write in first person from a teen-age girl's point of view. After all, I had three sisters and they had plenty of girls over to the house. Many evenings I sat with an ear to their closed bedroom door while they gossiped, so I considered myself enough of an authority to attempt a steamy story about a teen-aged girl's romance. I purchased several pulp magazines and read their stories then began to attempt my career as a wannabe pulp fiction writer.

Each night between customers, I would write longhand on filler notebook paper. The story was about a high school girl who had a crush on a guy named Tony, who repeatedly broke her heart—not particularly original, but I pieced together snippets of stories I had heard from my sisters and their girlfriends, embellished, adding my own touches that I thought would make the story more interesting and in line with what the publisher might be seeking. When the manuscript was finished I had it typed and sent it off to a pulp magazine publisher. Several weeks later I received a letter of acceptance with a contract. The pay was a nickel per word and the story became the sole property of the publisher. I signed the contract and returned it "airmail." Mail usually went by train unless one affixed additional postage and designated it "Air Mail." A few weeks after sending in the manuscript I received a check for about $300. I was a published author! The magazine, like so many others of that genre has long since gone out of business. I'm certain that fact had nothing to do with my story.

TEACHER, TEACHER

Despite my nocturnal writing and gas pumping ventures I was still able to fulfill my obligations as a sixth grade teacher. My school, Tendoy Elementary, was named for Chief Tendoy of the Lemhi Indian tribe. The school was bulging at the seams due to a Pocatello population growth spurt. To relieve the overcrowding a new school was built about a mile up the street and on the edge of town. It was named Edahow Elementary School. The name is rooted in local Native American folklore and means "light on the mountain." One such legend identifies the final resting place of Princess Edahow as the eerie ice mass found in the Shoshone Ice Caves, north of Twin Falls.

The naming of Edahow was felt to be in keeping with the district's tradition of naming schools after historical characters and events in Idaho history. Edahow Elementary School was not quite ready for occupancy at the start of the school year, thus I had a double sized class for the first few weeks of school. Aside from the problems created by overcrowding, the advantage was that I received cumulative folders of all 60 of the children and was able to see how each performed in class. When it was time to divide the group I got to determine who would stay and who would go. Of course I took the top 50 percent and sent the rest to Edahow. After the classes were separated, the initial heterogeneous group of 60 became a homogeneous group of 30 students. Not only were my students sharp academically, particularly in Math, but also they were very creative.

The students were given a great deal of leeway to allow for their creativity, and even wrote and performed their own Christmas show which could easily have been the forerunner of the comedy show, "Saturday Night Live". It was funny, clever, and every student in the class had a part. They even wrote spoof commercials to be given between scenes. While the theme of the birth of the Christ child was buried somewhere within, the show was performed in an excellent fashion, and of course, every parent believed their offspring to be the star. Even at that young age one could predict which students would become movers and shakers. Three stuck out in my mind; Skylar Rubel, whose mother was a teacher at the school and who I predicted would become a successful lawyer, Jeanine Goff who I predicted would become an upper level management leader, and Tina Watson, a tiny girl who even in the sixth grade showed agility and physical skill that would make me say she'd become a gymnast. It has been nearly 50 years since that special group of students shared a classroom with me and I have been unable to track any of them.

The class had such a proclivity for math that they had completed the entire math text by Thanksgiving holiday. I went to the District offices to get a set of seventh grade math books however, as I was loading them into my car, an assistant to the assistant superintendent (not the one who had hired me) asked me what I was doing, and I proudly told him that my sixth graders had completed their sixth grade math books and I planned to start them on the seventh grade books. He listened with a frown and said that would never do because if they learned seventh grade math in the sixth grade, what would be left to learn when they got to junior high? I chuckled. He was joking, right? Wrong! He was very serious and told me to return the books, as he turned on his heel and disappeared. Of course, I "forgot" to return the books and the class got through them by April. We spent the rest of the year learning Geometry from handouts and board work. I took the information from the single eighth grade math text I was able to appropriate from a junior high school math teacher. This time I refrained from sharing the math successes with the assistant to the assistant superintendent.

My principal was Ozzie Nelson. His first name was actually Gerald but he'd gone by the nickname Ozzie ever since the Ozzie and Harriet radio show, later to become a TV sitcom, came into being. We became fast friends and Ozzie would occasionally come to my classroom on days after I had spent the previous night at the service station. He would arrive after lunch and cover my class while I went home early to catch a nap before my tutoring sessions. He was a good principal, a good man and a good friend. He was from Montana and could fix anything mechanical. Neither of us were outdoorsmen but we decided to try pheasant hunting.

My father-in-law had given me a shotgun and a rifle. They were both old and I had never used them but Ozzie got an old shotgun from somewhere and I took the one I had never used, and we decided to become pheasant hunters. Since I worked the gas station Friday and Saturday nights, there would be two days during the week when I was off, and when I did not have go directly from the station to school. Occasionally on those days off Ozzie and I would go pheasant hunting in the early morning before school. Although I came from the Western Pennsylvania community of Clairton, setting for the "Deer Hunter" movie, I had never fired a weapon of any sort except for squirt guns, and one foray during my freshman year in college when a dorm mate took me home with him for Thanksgiving. We went deer hunting but I don't think I shot at anything. Ozzie was from Montana but had never been a serious hunter. We oiled up our shotguns for our new venture but after several treks into the Idaho wilderness we had shot at plenty of birds, but only winged one, disabling it, and Ozzie finished it off by whacking it with the butt of his shotgun. The gun went off when he struck the bird and we spent some time picking buckshot out of his side. Fortunately the worst injury was to his pride. My career as the great white pheasant hunter was a brief one.

STEVE'S NEW RIDE

During my time in Idaho my cousin, Steve Rudish, came to Rexburg, Idaho from Monaca, Pennsylvania, a community an hour away from Clairton and very similar to my hometown Steve played basketball and baseball at Ricks College in Rexburg, Idaho. Shortly after his arrival I took him with me on a weekend jaunt to Salt Lake City to show him the town and introduce him to my in-laws. While there, Steve wanted to shop for a cheap car, a "beater." We approached a used car lot and told the owner that Steve was on a basketball scholarship at Ricks and would likely complete his education on a basketball scholarship at BYU. The man's eyes lit up. He took us to a white '56 Ford Skyliner, which was in pretty good condition and he said, "You can have this car. I took it on trade and already made my money from it. All I ask is that when you play for BYU you get me some tickets." Steve agreed and drove off in a free car. I was suspicious. There couldn't have been "such a deal" that was legitimate, could there? But apparently there was. The owner of the car lot gave Steve a bill of sale showing the purchase price of $1.00 and Steve drove that car for several years.

A week or so after he had "purchased" the car Steve phoned me and said the brakes had gone out on the Ford. I told him that my principal, Ozzie Nelson could fix anything. That weekend I hitchhiked the 80 or so miles from Pocatello to Rexburg and picked up Steve and the car. We drove the car with NO BRAKES the entire way to Pocatello and Ozzie fixed the brakes. The adventure was not quite as scary as it might sound, for nearly the entire trip was on the freeway and we drove late at night when there were few cars on Interstate 15. We simply drove at 55 or so miles per hour and let the engine slow the car on downgrades. When we came to the exit in Pocatello we slowed the car as much as we could, took the off ramp at 10 mph or so, and coasted until the light at the bottom of the ramp turned green. Had we needed to come to a full stop there was always the emergency brake. From there it was only a block or so to Ozzie's house. Looking back, I'm not sure if it was cleverer than it was dangerous or more dangerous than clever.

MO'S BAR AND GRILL

Before going to the homes of the children I tutored I would often stop at a place called "Mo's Bar and Grill" for a sandwich after school. Bar owner Momir Baich was of the same ethnicity as was I; a fact that surprised me for most of the residents of Idaho were of Scandinavian decent and not Eastern European. However, Pocatello was fairly cosmopolitan as Idaho cities go. This was due to a World War II airfield on the edge of town that had been used for training pilots, the railroad that had housed many of its employees in Pocatello, and a factory that during the war had made large guns to be used as adjuncts to World War II vehicles.

Mo was an odd looking man and had a face that could have been in the funny papers, but he worked hard and had a good heart. Mo's wife Ann, the barmaid, food server, chief cook and bottle washer operated the food side while Mo ran the bar side. Her sandwiches were excellent as was the entire bar food menu. We became good friends and Mo's mantra was that he wanted to sell the business and get rid of the responsibility. He would almost daily remind me that, "You don't ever want to own a business. It owns you." We kept in touch after I left Idaho and I promised to try to find something for him in Vegas.

PREPARING FOR POST-POCATELLO

After being unable to find a teaching position in Utah, I had moved my wife to Pocatello and she had gotten a job as a secretary in the Admissions office at Idaho State University. We only had one car so I would drop her off in the morning, teach, and then pick her up after work. I usually got to her office before her workday was over and hung out near her office until she clocked out. Her office was next to the placement office and I always looked over the list to see who was coming to interview. When I saw Clark County, Nevada (Las Vegas) was scheduled to come to recruit teachers in February, I set myself up with an interview, especially after I saw their salary schedule—$8,300 per year vs. my current $5,300 in Idaho. If I could land a job in Vegas I would be rich! I would never have to work a second or third job again, or so I thought. Besides, by this time I was a fully licensed teacher, although I had never completed student teaching.

Bill Bietz, the principal at Clark High School in Las Vegas, was scheduled to interview me. Bill, an Idaho native and former Idaho football player, was running late with his appointments, and I had to leave to tutor (my second job). When he stepped out between interviews I caught him and asked if I could reschedule my interview for later. He suggested I come back at 9:00 p.m. when he'd finished all the other interviews and he would interview me last. At 9:00 p.m. I showed up and he invited me into his suite that also served as his interview room. His first question was, "Do you drink beer?"

I was taken aback. I knew Vegas had a heavily Mormon population but to ask such a question was outrageous. I couldn't imagine an interviewer from Utah or Idaho, both with mostly Mormon populations, asking such a question, let alone one from Las Vegas. Still, I wanted the job, but did not want to lie so I said, "Yes sir. I do have an occasional glass of beer but do not drink habitually."

His next question was, "What would you do if a kid told you to go to Hell?" I think I made up some sort of smart-aleck answer but could tell he was not paying attention. Those were the only questions in the interview. I assumed the interview was over and he needed to give me the bum's rush out of there when he next spoke.

He said, "Would you like one? A beer... I have a couple of six-packs on ice in the bathroom tub and after a long day of talking I'm dying for one." We had a few beers, made small talk, and he told me I would be placed on the Clark County School District Personnel Department "Hire" list and to call the personnel office in April for my assignment.

A BRIEF STINT IN UTAH

Shortly after that interview, my then father-in-law, who had a heart attack before we moved to Idaho, took a turn for the worse. My wife's cousin, Reed Beckstead, was the superintendent of the Jordan School District, south of Salt Lake City. The family prevailed upon him to offer me a job so we could be near her father during his last days. I phoned the Clark County School District Personnel Department and they agreed to keep me on the inactive list until the following year.

The school year in Pocatello ended, and we packed our things and moved to the Salt Lake City area where I taught for one year in the Jordan School District's Midvale Elementary School. During that year, in the springtime, the principal called me into his office and said, "Andy, we really like your leadership abilities and would like to consider you for a position as principal. You have all the qualities we are looking for but before we could make such an appointment you would have to become active in 'the church'"

I did not break stride but said, "Thank you Brother Ashman. Let me go home and study and pray about it." (That is Utah code for "I'll probably do it but need a little time"). I went home, called the Clark County School District Personnel Department, and told them to activate my file. Within 30 minutes my phone rang and principal Galen Good hired me sight unseen as a sixth grade teacher at Rex Bell Elementary School in Las Vegas. I finished the school year in Utah, tied up loose ends over the summer (my father-in-law had passed away by this time) and planned to move to Vegas in August.

By this time we had been married for three years and were childless. This was a sign of something amiss in the Mormon culture, and my wife's relatives and friends were pressuring her unmercifully because she was childless and not pregnant. As for me, whenever anybody had the audacity to ask me why we were childless I gave a flippant answer such as, "My wife had failed the blood test and syphilis often makes one infertile." They rarely asked a second time. But I was sensitive to the pressure she was under so I went to her family's lawyer, Vic Sager, an elderly gentleman with whom I had become friendly. Vic the lawyer took his breakfast each morning in the Midvale bowling alley across from Dorothea's Flower Shop and just up the street from Midvale Elementary School. There he would hold court with assorted clients and friends before starting his workday. I stopped by one morning and told him that my wife and I were interested in adopting and that we had placed our names on the Catholic Welfare list and been told it was a 3-year wait. We'd placed our names on the Utah welfare list and been told it was a 7-year wait. I asked him if, as an attorney and trusted Latter Day Saint elder, he knew of any situations in which a baby might become available for adoption through the church network. He pulled out a pad and pencil and asked, "Gender? Hair Color? Eye color?" I him that eye and hair color did not matter and I would sort of like a boy, but that was just 51-49 and either would be fine.

One month before we were to move to Vegas, Vic called and said that we needed to be at a hospital in Tustin, California by 10:00 a.m. the following day to pick up our baby boy. He was the product of a high school romance. The girl was LDS. We got a complete dossier on her but she knew nothing about us—I always thought that seemed unfair. We borrowed a car crib from Elise, my wife's cousin, and drove all night to Orange County, California's Tustin Hospital where we picked up our 3-day old boy, whom we named Andrew Richard, Jr. After a visit with my brother-in-law (Sherma's older brother by 18 years) and his 12 children, we drove back to Salt Lake City. Nine months and two weeks after our son was born, Sherma had a baby girl at Las Vegas Sunrise Hospital. We named her Crystal Michelle, after nobody in particular. We just liked the sound of the name. When people who didn't realize the first child had been adopted asked how it happened that we had two children so close together I'd say, "Never get a private room in the hospital."

A LAS VEGAS EDUCATION

Because I'd taught under contract for four years prior to coming to Las Vegas, (one year in Pennsylvania, two in Idaho, and one in Utah) I had not been required to student teach. I discovered that in most states, if one teach three years or more under contract student teaching is waived. Also by this time I had teaching credentials and excellent evaluations for the elementary grades in Pennsylvania, Idaho, Utah, and Nevada. An elementary license in Nevada includes K-8, all subjects. I find it ironic that although I never student taught, I became a master teacher a few weeks into my career and would eventually be in charge of the student teaching program at Nova Southeastern University.

After picking up our three-day old son in California, we returned to Utah to tie up loose ends, then drove to Vegas in late August. We had two cars by this time, a 1966 Pontiac Bonneville that I had purchased new just before leaving

Pocatello, and the trusty Rambler convertible that I had driven from Pennsylvania and driven in Idaho for two years with expired tags. The drive to Las Vegas was a cool one through the mountains of Southern Utah. Neither car had air conditioning but we did have a month-old baby who was fine as we drove in the cool pristine air of Southern Utah. However, by the time we got to Mesquite, the first stop in Nevada, the temperature had soared to 110 and neither the baby nor the adults were adjusting well. One of my wife's cousins was driving my Rambler convertible and I was driving the Pontiac Bonneville while pulling the biggest U-Haul trailer available. As the temperature continued to soar, about 10 miles north of Mesquite on an upgrade, the Bonneville began to overheat. The big V-8 engine was not built to pull a fully loaded trailer up a steep grade in 110-plus degree heat. I pulled over and thankfully a Recreational Vehicle driven by a young couple pulled up behind me to see if they could help. It must have been 115 by then and the baby was fussy, as were the adults. I sent Sherma, the baby, and her cousin on ahead, and said I would meet them in Vegas. I had already pre-rented an air-conditioned apartment so all they had to do was get the key from the manager and they would have cool air.

The RV driver was used to crossing the desert and carried plenty of water. Once we got the Pontiac cooled down he followed me another 20 or so miles until it overheated again. As we waited to get the car cooled down again and add more water we chatted. He told me that he was a struggling actor and had just been in his first movie—a small part. They planned to visit his wife's family in Las Vegas then continue to Los Angeles for his next movie. They were so nice. He followed me all the way to Las Vegas where the freeway ended at Lamb Boulevard (in those days) then they headed for her parents' home. I had never heard of him as an actor until much later when I saw the unforgettable mug of the actor, Bruce Dern.

TAXI, TAXI!

I arrived in Las Vegas August 1968 and had rented an apartment on Fairfield Street. It was one of many apartment complexes where transient Las Vegas workers lived. From my balcony I was able to see the time and temperature sign atop the Sathara Hotel, and on the day of our arrival it read 117. The Fairfield neighborhood was a safe, clean, working class neighborhood, but has since deteriorated. Crime has increased dramatically and by the 1980s the media began to be refer to the area as "Naked City."

The apartment was conveniently located to my school, Rex Bell Elementary School. Galen Good was the principal at the school. The school was named for movie cowboy Rex Bell, who had been married to the "it girl" Clara Bow, the sexy siren movie star of the Great Depression era. They lived on a ranch near Searchlight, located in the southern tip of Nevada. The marriage of the two stars produced Rex Bell, Jr.

who later became a good friend as well as the local District Attorney. Searchlight is also noted as the place where Senate Majority Leader Harry Reid grew up.

The apartment was close enough to the school for me to come home for lunch. Sherma did not work outside the home, but tended our little son, so we were able to have lunch together regularly. One day at lunch she said, "Guess what, Daddy?" That was how she announced her pregnancy. After three years of non-conception and the adoption of little A.R. we were going to have a baby the old fashioned way. Our two children could be described as, "We bought one and built one."

Sherma had been anemic from time to time but fortunately she remained healthy throughout the pregnancy. The school district provided good insurance coverage and my out of pocket expenses were only $500 for the birth, which I paid to the hospital in advance. The pregnancy was not a difficult one but her labor went on for close to 12 hours. I made the mistake of calling Dorthea and telling her that I was taking Sherma to the hospital. The mistake was that the long labor gave Dorthea time to race to the airport in Salt Lake City, fly to Vegas, and catch a taxi to the hospital.

Sherma had been in considerable pain and discomfort during labor and the doctors had just gotten her calmed. The possibility of Caesarian was not considered, as the doctors did not think it necessary. Just as Sherma was getting calm, Dorthea burst into the room screaming, "Oh, my baby, my baby, you are in such bad condition!" That woman could disrupt a peace conference. She was far and away the push-iest, most manipulating, disagreeable, dare I say, obnoxious, person I had ever known. The doctors attempted to usher her into the next room but she put up a protest, accusing them of torturing her baby girl. Eventually, they threatened to have her removed by Security if she didn't calm down. She finally shut up and shortly thereafter Sherma delivered Crystal.

After the delivery, when Sherma was in recovery, Dorthea asked what we planned to name the baby. I told her that I liked the name Crystal and Sherma liked Michelle so we decided to name her Crystal Michelle. She wrinkled up her face and said, "What ugly names. I thought you might name her after me. You could still do that, you know." I said nothing although my impulse was for a snappy comeback that burned in my mouth.

Now that Sherma was a full time mom with two babies, and I was supporting a family of four with only one income I did a fiscal assessment. With my debt from my first year teaching not yet paid in full, I decided to seek a second job. From my apartment balcony I could see Whittlesea Taxi Company. I walked over one day and asked if they needed any drivers. Jim Bell, who had recently moved to Vegas to work for his uncle Vic Whittlesea, hired me and I told him I was a teacher and was only interested in driving part time. He said that he did not hire part time employees and he did not care what I did on my own time, but if I wanted to work full time and drive nights, he would hire me. I agreed. He asked me if I had any experience driving taxi and I lied and said yes, that I'd driven for the Clairton Cab Company in my hometown. I knew there was no way to check this as the Hrbrosky family that had owned the Clairton Cab Company had closed it, and there was no local taxi service in the town.

It took a few days to get a Sheriff's card, a requirement for all Strip workers that included a background check, a health certificate to prove I was still alive, and a chauffer's driving license. Once all the pre-driving requirements were completed, my "training" consisted of riding along with a seasoned company driver for a couple of hours; then I was on my own.

The company maintained the taxis. Drivers were not required to "rent" their cabs as in other cities. Instead, a driver simply was assigned a shift with a designated cab and left the garage with it. For the next nine hours he was on his own. Each time a fare got in the taxi, the flag on the meter was thrown and the meter clicked off so much per mile and so much per minute. At the end of the shift, all the money, or "book," excluding tips, was tallied and turned in to the office. Drivers were paid 50 percent of "book" less taxes and required deductions, and paychecks were generated weekly. Some drivers wasted time during their shifts, others spent their shifts trying to hustle for hookers, and others approached the job with a laid back attitude. Not me. I was there to work and I soon figured out which hotel taxi lines moved the fastest, what times to "play" particular hotels (show breaks were good times), and other tricks of the trade. As a result I was consistently one of the highest earners and soon got the notice of Jim Bell and his assistant, Charlie Ford, another transplanted Pittsburgher. That notice brought me better cabs and other subtle perks such as working weekends as a dispatcher. It was also the genesis of a friendship with Jim Bell.

I had very little seniority so I was assigned to be an "extra" driver, which meant I showed up at a designated time and was assigned the cab of a regular driver who had called in sick or otherwise did not show up for work. The show-up time for shift assignments was 2:30 p.m. Of course, at that time I was teaching school, so I took my kids to recess at 2:15. Another teacher would watch them for me while I ran over to Whittlesea, which was located just around the corner from Rex Bell Elementary School, and picked up my shift, which would be scheduled to start sometime between 4:30 and 6:00 p.m. Then I would race back to school, finish my teaching day, go home and freshen up, and drive my assigned taxi for nine hours.

Before my taxi days, however, there was another interlude. When I first got to Las Vegas, I went to the 7-11 on Teddy Drive and Sahara Avenue, around the corner from Rex Bell Elementary School, and told the owner that I taught at the nearby school, and asked if he needed help. The owner was Ed Camilli who had just moved to Las Vegas to retire. He bought the 7-11 franchise after selling his business in New Castle, Pennsylvania. He hired me on the spot and I worked the 7-11 from after school until I closed the store at 11:00 pm. But I was not making enough money there so I started driving cab. However, on my days off from cab and school I continued to work at the 7-11.

When I started driving taxi, after only a few weeks in town, I had no clue where anything was located in Vegas so I would go to the Sahara taxi stand on the north end of the Strip, pick up a fare who would usually give me the name of a hotel destination. I would drive down the Strip until I saw the hotel and pull in, drop off the fare and head for the Tropicana or Hacienda at the south end of the Strip. Thus I only went one way, back and forth on the Strip until I learned where all the hotels were located. I would take an occasional fare off the Strip, usually a dealer or dancer who got off work and needed a ride home. They would give me directions and that's how I learned the town.

Taxi driving was a different world than anything I had ever done. By this time I had delivered papers, been a box boy in a super market, worked in the BYU library, bought and sold used cars, taken students across country for a fee, worked in a steel mill, taught school, tutored, pumped gas, delivered flowers, and clerked in a 7-11. Life as a night shift taxi driver in Las Vegas was a completely new and different experience. I have always loved the night and I loved driving cab. I loved the hookers, the dealers, the high rollers, the drunks, and even the vice cops. In fact, the vice cops had a ruse. They would walk out of a hotel in plain clothes posing as a tourist and ask a cab driver to fix them up with a hooker. The driver often did so, since many call girls and hookers gave their phone numbers to taxi drivers, and they would pay a very handsome tip if the driver set her up with a date.

Many drivers ran hookers on the side and those who did so rarely drove their shifts. Once a driver took the vice cops to the hooker both would be arrested, her for prostitution and the driver for pandering. I could never understand how a taxi driver could not recognize the vice cops who stuck out of the mainstream tourist genre like a sore thumb, with their wrinkled suits and holster bulge under their suit coat.

There were other ways to earn money as a taxi driver besides earning half of the meter registry. Of course, one could hustle for hookers, but the chances of being arrested and ruining my career as an educator dissuaded me from considering that option. There were still plenty of opportunities for "side money." This included taking a fare to a particular restaurant, nightclub, or even hotel that paid a "spiff" to the driver for the business. One would escort the fare into the establishment and hand the maître 'd a business card with the taxi number and company phone number, and say, "Please take care of my friends, and call me if they need a ride back to the Strip." The taxi number would be noted and afterward the driver would stop by to pick up his "spiff." At the time the going rate was $2 per person for most places. The Gold Key Motel on the corner of the Strip and Convention Center Drive was one of my favorites to take tourists in need of a room, as they paid $4 for the guest's first night's visit and $3 for each additional night.

Although it is illegal to use anything but government-printed legal tender as legal tender, casino chips were often used in Las Vegas. Each hotel-casino minted their own chips and for the most part no casino would accept a chip from competitor's casino. But that did not stop the ancillary industries such as taxis, limos, hookers, hairdressers, bartenders, and the like to use chips as currency. In fact there is an old story about Our Lady of Las Vegas, a Catholic Church just off the Strip. As the story goes, the priest would tell the congregation of mostly visitors each Sunday that his church accepted chips as donations. The story further goes that the chips are brought to a nearby monastery where monks separated them by casino and cashed them in to the respective casinos. The priest would say that the monks who did this toil for God were a special order called "chip-monks."

How much could a taxi driver make in an average night? My "book" usually averaged between $50 and $70 so my daily pay was half of that less deductions. I might average another $20 - $30 per night in tips, and $10 - $15 in spiffs. My average earnings would be about $60 per night or $300 per week; nearly double what I earned teaching school. There is no better feeling than going to work with empty pockets and coming home with money from tips. During holidays and big conventions drivers were permitted to drive 12 hour shifts to accommodate the influx of tourists and those shifts yielded considerably more money. Also, the union or the company always had a deal with a grocery store to give free Christmas and Thanksgiving turkeys to all drivers.

LAS VEGAS UNDERGROUND

An interesting phenomenon about Las Vegas at the time was the underground portion of the economy. Most who took part in that underground economy worked in large part for tips; Cocktail and food waitresses, card dealers, taxi drivers, valet car parkers, hair stylists, and many of the others who depended on tips for the majority of their income were given those tips directly from customers. Dealers pooled their tips. That is, whenever any dealer was given a tip it was placed in a "pot" then divided among all dealers. That way, those on the night shift, where tips were often greater, and those on the day shift, split their tips equally. But many tip recipients shared their tips in other ways. The dealer tipped the boxman, the cocktail waitress tipped the bartender, the food waitress tipped the cooks and the hostesses, and so forth. Tips often exceeded salaries and were an integral part of the economy. Of course, if tips were reported to the IRS at all, only the tiniest of portions were reported. That was the process until the IRS cracked down and demanded that individual and hotel records be kept.

Other parts of the underground Las Vegas economy employed people who received no formal paychecks. Prostitution is banned in only two counties in Nevada; Clark (Las Vegas) and Washoe (Reno). There is no such statute in any of the other Nevada counties that addresses prostitution. Hence, the image is that it is legal in Vegas and Reno when in fact it is illegal but often is winked at. Because of the clandestine nature of the business and payment, one would think there are no rules, but in point of fact, there are rules that are followed to the letter or "working girls" will find their business will dry up.

Not all prostitutes are created equal in the eyes of the profession. Streetwalkers occupy the lowest rung on the ladder. They often have pimps but occasionally are freelancers who come to town during large conventions or occasionally might be housewives who have gambled the rent money and need a quick financial fix. Some turn tricks to support a drug habit.

The next step up are the working girls who do not have pimps per se, but whose contact information is in the possession of valets, maître d's, bellmen, taxi drivers, bartenders, and the like. Because those professions are most likely to come in contact with men looking for "a little company," a quick call to an available working girl will do the trick, as it were. The working girl transacts the business and collects the fee, then kicks back 40 percent to the person who arranged the date.

The highest paid and top level of hookers are referred to as call girls or escorts. They work on referral only and their contact information is given only to the hotel employees who come in contact with high rollers referred to in the trade as "whales." The "commission" however, is still the standard 40 percent.

With no pun intended, plenty of people look to get a piece of the prostitute, especially the top-level girls. The higher the price for the services, the better the merchandise must be. Clothing and jewelry for the escort or call girl must be expensive and top-of-the line. Ditto makeup. Since the stakes are so high and so much money changes hands, there must be as little evidence as possible of her existence. That means an apartment rented, usually under an assumed name, and paid for in cash. No car or traceable property ownership so she must travel by taxi or hotel limo. Everybody in the business knows who the doctors are who will provide prescriptions and cosmetic surgery, as needed, all transactions done in cash of course. It is a fascinating underground culture.

During my tenure as a taxi driver I met many working girls, hookers and call girls. Nearly everyone had the same goal – to make a big score, save a bunch of money, then return to Hoboken or Poughkeepsie or Peoria or from whence she came, and live the rest of her life as a respectable housewife or professional woman. In nearly every instance, however, they never seemed to achieve their goal. They would either succumb to the fast life or the drugs, or the good times. I only saw one example of a person that was able to stay true to her plans. She had a Master's degree from Columbia University in English Literature and wrote poetry. I first picked her up on a radio call when she was headed for a client. We talked on the way to the hotel and I told her I was a schoolteacher and Psychology major who also wrote poetry. Thereafter whenever she called the taxi company she requested my number (these are called "personal calls" and are common in the taxi business).

We became friends, exchanged poetry, and edited one another's writings. She was very focused on her goal and had a designated amount of time to fulfill her plans as well as a financial goal. She saved her money and kept the cash in a safety deposit box of a private security company. Once she met the threshold she desired, she disappeared and presumably returned home to complete her career in higher education. I never heard from her after she left and I did not know her real name or where she lived before and after her time in Vegas, but I did have one big adventure with her.

It was a slow night and I was sitting in my cab, fourth up on the Thunderbird taxi stand. I saw a man walk out of the hotel and ask the first driver something. The driver shook his head and the man walked to the second and third taxi. Both had the same response, shaking their head. When he got to my cab he asked, "Habla usted Espanol?" (Do you speak Spanish?)

I said "Si," and he explained that he was from Spain and in town on a convention with other Spaniards, none of whom spoke much English. He'd like some company and did I know of anybody who would spend some time with him. My first thought was that he might be a vice cop trying to trap me but his Spanish was so crisp with a Castilian lilt that I was certain he was really from Spain. I said I knew of a girl that might fit the bill then asked for his room number and told him I'd call her and let her know.

He returned to the hotel and I went inside to the pay phone and phoned the only call girl I knew—my poetry-sharing friend with the master's degree from Columbia. She said she was not busy and I picked her up in my taxi and took her to the hotel. I gave her time to get up to the room and phoned to make sure everything was all right. She assured me it was and I asked if she spoke Spanish. She laughed and said no but there was a universal language that they both understood. Duh.

She also told me several of his friends were en route to his and nearby rooms so she was having several of her uh colleagues come by to join the party. I wished her well, parked the cab around back and went to the deli to grab some lunch.

HIGH SHERIFFS AND POLICE COMING AFTER ME

When I returned to my cab after an enjoyable lunch, and began to leave, the scene suddenly looked like somebody had just won a huge jackpot. Red lights were blinking everywhere and spotlights were shining on me. What seemed like the entire sheriffs department was surrounding my taxi. A gruff cop said, "Get out of that car, boy."

I had assumed that this was a setup and I was in trouble for sending a girl to the room of a vice cop, but they gave no such indication and besides, these were all patrol cars and not unmarked vice cars. Several cops opened all the doors of my cab including the trunk and began going through my trip sheets and papers (I often brought my school work with me to work on in my taxi during the slow times), ripped the back seat out of the car, and were clearly looking for SOMETHING! Drugs perhaps?

A cop said, "Empty your pockets on the hood of the cab. What is your cab doing parked here?" And I told him that I'd been having dinner in the café.

I asked what they were looking for and the one goon in a police uniform said to me, "Shut up, boy. We'll ask the questions."

I became irritated, particularly as they had my lessons strewn all over the inside of the cab and I said, as politely as I could, "Sir, if you'll tell me what you're looking for I'll be happy to help you find it."

With that the goon slammed me against the car and said, "I told you, boy, shut the fuck up or my friend here (tapping the billy club on his belt) will start doing the talking."

My papers, including school papers I had been grading and the trip sheet that had sat next to me on the bench seat were now scattered around the inside of the car. The goon again told me to empty my pockets and put the contents on the hood of the car. I told him I had already done that and he growled. A salt-and-pepper haired sergeant picked up my key ring from the hood of the car and asked me to identify what each of the keys went to. I guess cab drivers did not typically carry a large, fully stocked key ring on their person. I slowly went through each key, my house key, car keys, key to the school, key to my classroom, key to the lock on the fence around the playing field. The sergeant looked at me oddly and I said, "I'm a schoolteacher. I teach the sixth grade at Rex Bell Elementary School during the day and I drive this taxi at night as a second job to support my family.

I cannot understand why the police department, particularly that GOON over there," as I pointed to the one who had been threatening me, "is threatening me."

The sergeant then took a fatherly posture and said, "Well, Mr. Nixon, clearly we've made a mistake. But you see there has been a series of thefts from hotel rooms. We suspect that some cab drivers might be involved, and when Security reported your cab was parked around the back of the building we thought we might have had a suspect. But I can see that is not the case and I apologize for any inconvenience."

In truth I was able to see how a taxi parked behind a hotel for an extended period of time would be a suspect in a theft ring. Prior to hotels having plastic card keys as they do today, most hotel room keys were large, metal objects. Often a fare would hand a room key to the driver, who might toss it on the dashboard, and as a courtesy, drop it off when next he stopped by the hotel. It would be easy for the driver to pocket the key and return to the hotel to burgle the room. If a fare to the airport gave his key to me, I would ask if he had any casino chips left over that he'd like to sell for 50 cents on the dollar. The chips would be worthless to him back in Sheboygan or Shreveport or Shangri-La, so I might offer to buy $10 worth of chips for $5 and make $5 for my trouble. More often than not the fare would simply give me his leftover chips as a tip.

Still, I was mad as Hell for the way I was treated, especially by the goon cop, and when the sergeant said I was free to go I said, "You know, many of my students come from working families. They call police pigs and demean them and I have always tried to explain the purpose for the police and the good things they do. But today I experienced that goon who abused me, tore my cab apart and left the mess for me to clean up, and threatened me with violence. Once you discovered I was educated it was all 'Mr.' and 'Sir.' Had this been my only contact with the police I would probably share the view that many of the parents of my students have—that you deserve to be called pigs."

He said nothing more but returned to his car and left me in the parking lot to clean up the mess his gang had left.

REAPING THE SPOILS

The following day, a Saturday, my poetry buddy phoned and asked me to come by. It was time to exchange poetry so I brought some I had recently written and headed for her apartment. She thanked me for the previous night and handed me an envelope brimming with cash. I told her I did not want the money but that I phoned her simply because she was a friend. She said, no, business is business and she had collected the percentage from all the girls who had come by and worked that night. She couldn't very well return the money, so I might as well take it.

Ok. I did. I went directly to a realtor and used the money for the down payment on my first house.

TAXI DRIVING'S DOWN SIDES

I only had one direct encounter with the vice cops. They got into my cab posing as tourists and asked if I could set them up with a hooker. I asked them if they had ever been to Vegas before and they said no. I knew exactly who they were so I said, "Sure!"

They said, "Let's go."

I turned onto Sahara and after a few minutes one of them said, "Where are we going?"

I said, "To Pahrump—a place called the Chicken Ranch. It is in Nye County and prostitution is legal there." Oh were they pissed! They made me stop immediately and got out of the cab on the spot. Apparently another unmarked car was following us and the two vice cops got into it. But I made them pay the fare first—no tip—and I had to give them a receipt.

Driving taxi was not without its dangers. There was the

ever-present possibility of being robbed at gunpoint. As a hedge against being robbed, I always kept a blank trip sheet (in which each trip had to be logged along with the amount of cash collected for that trip) on a clipboard. My plan was that if I were ever held up I would show the trip sheet and say I had just come to work. But I was never robbed, although there was a time when a person got in my cab and I was certain he meant to rob me. I just picked up bad vibes from his furtive movements. He sat in the corner where I was unable to see him in my mirror. I engaged him in conversation, letting him know that I was a schoolteacher and had a family and this was my first trip of the evening. When I stopped at a traffic light he jumped out of the cab and disappeared. I was certain that I had just talked my way out of being robbed.

The scariest moment for me was when I was given a radio call to pick up a passenger several miles out of town on the way to Lake Mead. She lived in a trailer park and was to go for some sort of medical treatment. It was a "welfare call;" meaning I did not get paid by the passenger, but received scrip that I turned in for money, as the state had an account with the taxi company. I was given her first name, Sarah.

When I pulled up in front of the trailer, a man was sitting on the porch. He apparently had recent throat surgery and had some sort of screen where his larynx should have been. I said, "I'm looking for Sarah." He motioned me into the trailer and we walked to the back where a woman, presumably Sarah, was asleep in bed. He grabbed her by the ankle and flipped her onto the floor, then pointed at her and myself, suggesting, I guess, that we were somehow involved. I tried to get past him to leave but he became more agitated and as we got to the kitchen he picked up a knife from the sink and lifted it to slice me. I punched him in the throat and ran out the door and into the cab. He ran onto the porch and simulated a rifle shooting at me. His throat was bleeding but he did not seem to notice. I peeled out of the lot and drove to the edge of the park where I had to stop as I was trembling so badly. When I called the dispatcher and told her what had happened she said, "Oh I see you met her crazy husband." That was it. No further explanation.

POCATELLO TO LAS VEGAS, 2.0

Once I was settled in Las Vegas my friend in Pocatello, Mo Baich, put his tavern in Idaho up for sale. The place sold and he and Ann packed up their two children and headed for Las Vegas. I helped them find an apartment near the Sahara Hotel, close to where I lived when I first moved to Las Vegas. Ann was ecstatic at being a stay-at-home (or more accurately stay-at-apartment) mom. Mo, however, was frustrated at not being able to immediately find work in the hospitality industry. I suggested he try taxi driving as I was doing. By this time Jim Bell, nephew of Vic Whittlesea and manager of the taxi company and I had become friends. I was certain he would hire Mo but Mo was reluctant. He had never driven taxi (nor had I prior to becoming a professional driver, which I pointed out to Mo) and did he not think he would like it. But when I explained that it would just be until he got something permanent, and it would pay the rent, and driving taxi in Vegas was a lark since one needed to only learn one street—the Strip—he reluctantly agreed to try it—just for a short time.

Mo fell in love with life as a taxi driver. He used his talent as an excellent conversationalist (a talent that had served him well as a bartender) to increase his tips, and he discovered, as had I, that one could live on day-to-day tips and save his weekly paychecks for the big expenses. He eventually was moved from the "extra board" to a regular shift, and drove cab until the day he died – literally. Mo had been living in Vegas and driving taxi for more than a decade. His children had grown and married and Ann continued her life not having to work outside the home. Mo's routine was to work the Strip for the first half of his shift, then drive to the downtown area where he would park the taxi in the shade of the Greyhound Bus Depot and have lunch at the Union Plaza (a hotel that had been built on the site of the old Union Pacific Railroad Station). After lunch he would rest in his cab for a while, perhaps taking a nap before completing his shift. One day after lunch he returned to his cab, closed his eyes, and never awoke. I am certain Mo died a happy man.

Vic Whittlesea, an entrepreneur and longtime Nevada resident, owned Whittlesea Taxi. He lived in Las Vegas and owned taxi fleets in Las Vegas, Reno, and Sacramento as well as rental properties, apartments, and a host of other revenue-generating activities. In the mid 1960s, Vic, a single man with no children, invited his nephew Jim Bell to come to Las Vegas and learn the business. Jim had grown up in Montana and with the hopes of working in his uncle's business, had attended Business College for a couple of years in Chicago. Jim married his high school sweetheart, Carol and moved to Las Vegas to work for Uncle Vic.

Vic had come up the hard way and while he was willing to turn the business over to his nephew a little at a time, he was insistent that Jim learn it from the ground up. That meant starting by working in the garage and cleaning the lavatories. He put Jim on a humble salary with a weekly draw but picked up all his living expenses. This suited Jim fine, but soon he and Carol started a family, and the weekly draw was barely enough for the incidentals needed to run the house. As their children and Jim's career grew, Carol pressed Jim to ask his uncle for a raise, insisting that as a manager he should be earning more than he did as a trainee. But Jim's response would always be, "Some day the business will be mine. I can't pester him for more money. You'll just have to make do."

Jim and Carol separated and got back together several times until they could no longer agree on his pay schedule and whatever other differences they might have had. A few weeks after the divorce was final Vic passed away, leaving nearly his entire estate to Jim. Jim and Carol remained friends and she took a job with the limousine service. Jim, however, remained one of the town's most eligible bachelors the rest of his life.

TAXIS AND LIMOS

As an atypical taxi driver I noticed many things in Las Vegas that might have escaped the eyes of others. First was the totally different life that existed once the sun went down and the neon lights came up. The city came alive. Joe and Jane Normal became Pete and Paula Party. The energy and excitement of Las Vegas at night was a hundred times that of the same village during the day. I loved the sights and sounds and smells of the night. I loved watching movies being filmed in the downtown area and on the Strip. I loved the gamblers – the few winners and the many losers, and I loved the hookers, the dealers, the boxmen, and the entertainers who would ride in my cab. My fares included Sammy Davis, Jr. and wife, Lucille Ball and hubby, and others from the rich and famous set. Vegas nights were enchanting and I would become enchanted every night.

I also noticed several things about the business end

of Vegas. One was that there existed only one Limousine Company and it had only four cars. This seemed odd to me in a land of high rollers. Occasionally a limo would drive from Los Angeles or Phoenix, and some hotels had their own limos, but for the most part, the community depended on one limo Company and its four limos. I was curious to see how taxis and limos were licensed in Clark County and discovered that taxis were limited in number but limousines were not. Each taxi company was assigned a designated number of medallions, one of which must be affixed to each cab, thereby regulating the number of taxis permitted to operate in the county at a given time. Regulations for limousines were much more lax. Each company was required to have a certificate, which did not restrict the number of limos in service at any given time. There was only one such certificate in Clark County. Hotels were exempt and did not need a certificate but could only service their own properties.

Jim Bell and I had become friends. On the occasional Saturday that I did not drive he might invite me to go with him to Lake Mead and ride his boat. On one such outing I expressed to him that, admittedly, I knew little about the transportation business in Las Vegas but it seemed to me that more business existed than was being served. I suggested that his uncle purchase the existing limousine company and put more limos on the street.

Jim was more interested in having a quiet beer than in listening to me and he said, "Why don't I set up a meeting with you and my uncle and have you explain it to him." We did so and I explained the situation from my point of view to Uncle Vic, including what I had learned about licensing.

Bob Weeks was a high profile entrepreneur in Las Vegas. He was single and had a rich girlfriend who disappeared. Although her body was never found he was convicted of her murder. Long before that conviction Bob Weeks owned the lone limo company in Southern Nevada. Vic bought him out, probably for more than Bob thought it was worth. Vic started with the four limos but soon added another 12 then 12 more, and finally, after another 12. When the fleet reached 40 the business need seemed to be addressed. Vic asked me what I wanted for the idea and I said, "For you to be successful and for me to drive limousines." He gave me a substantial bonus and I became one of the first limo drivers. Instead of paying a portion of the taxi "book," limo drivers were paid an hourly wage. That meant that during those long winter evenings when business was slow, we still got paid, and when business was good, we made much better tips than taxi drivers. It was a win-win. Although driving remained my second income, education continued as my primary profession. However I would be lying if I said I did not have occasional thoughts of chucking the teaching profession and becoming a limo driver and businessman.

THE ACCIDENTAL HIGH SCHOOL TEACHER

After a year teaching elementary school in Nevada, the state Board of Education deemed Psychology to be a teaching subject at the high school level. I applied to teach Psychology and was hired at Western High School in Las Vegas and spent the next three years having the time of my life teaching Psychology and working with high school kids during the day, but still driving limo at night and on weekends. At age 24, I was teaching kids just a few years younger than me and I often felt more like a peer than a teacher. My high school years as a Psychology teacher were much more rewarding than those as a student at Clairton High School.

In addition to teaching Psychology during the day and driving limo nights and weekends I was also teaching Behind-the-Wheel Driver Education at Western High School. I was simply spending too much time chasing the dollar and not enough time at home. My marriage ended after five years and Sherma and the kids returned to Utah. We had begun the marriage as two immature kids and for the most part we were still pretty immature. However I was able to be out in the world interacting with others but she was sentenced to house arrest with two babies, both in diapers. We did not fight or argue; our marriage, which had started by default, dissolved.

The divorce was amicable. The judge set the child support and I had worked out a plan to divide our possessions. The equity in the house was determined and I sent monthly checks to her for that in addition to child support. I am proud to say that I never missed a child support payment. I have had many jobs, but Deadbeat Dad was never one of them.

GETTING ON WITH MY LIFE

After the 1970 divorce Sherma returned to Utah, the flower shops and her domineering mother. Dorthea remarried a wonderful man, who also preceded her in death. As she aged her mind became less sharp. She ignored obligations and tax deadlines until the feds threatened to shutter her shops. Sherma saved them by taking ownership and pledging her own house as collateral against the back taxes. Dorothea continued to deteriorate mentally and Sherma eventually became her caretaker.

I moved on with my life as well. I kept the house and started a Masters Degree program through Northern Arizona University (NAU). Their program was specifically designed for Clark County School District teachers. The NAU program was a unique concept designed to draw teachers from the University of Nevada, Las Vegas Master's program to the NAU Master of Education program. Northern Arizona

University is in Flagstaff, a several hour drive from Las Vegas. NAU mitigated the distance by sending faculty members to Kingman, Arizona, a 100-mile, ninety-minute trek from Las Vegas, and the home of cowboy actor Andy Devine. Classes were taught at Kingman High School. Educators from the Las Vegas area would make the drive to Kingman Friday after school, attend class Friday night, all day Saturday, and Sunday morning, and then return to Las Vegas Sunday afternoon. Four such weekends equaled one three credit graduate class. Friday after class and Saturday nights were available for socializing, although there was little to do in Kingman. The running joke was that the only bar in Kingman had burned to the ground leaving 300 people homeless.

In addition to taking classes in Kingman, two summers in residence at the main campus in Flagstaff was required. By following that regimen one could complete a Masters program in two years without having to leave the local school district. There were other benefits to the NAU program. Summers are hot in Las Vegas but beautiful in Flagstaff, and the entire venture was tax deductible. Tuition was quite reasonable and no out of state tuition was required, so the entire program at NAU was less expensive than completing a masters degree at UNLV. Teachers flocked to the NAU program, and the schedule allowed me to earn a graduate degree while continuing my extra jobs and reducing my debt, as well as maintaining my financial obligation to my children.

While in summer school at Flagstaff I met Patti Sepich, also a teacher in Clark County. Patti's parents were Las Vegas pioneers. Her father, Frank Sepich, had come to Las Vegas at the urging of friends in the mid-1950s. He had worked at International Harvester in Canton, Illinois for years, but strikes and work stoppages made that job tenuous, much like the steel industry in Pennsylvania. Friends of his family had moved to Las Vegas and wrote letters to Frank telling him of the building boom taking place in Las Vegas. Frank boarded a train in Illinois, which arrived at the downtown Fremont Las Vegas train depot at 10:00 a.m. on a beautiful, warm morning in November. By noon of the same day, Frank had obtained work as a carpenter helping to build the Mint, then other downtown hotels. He worked continuously while his friends and neighbors in Illinois continued to endure cold weather and work stoppages. Patti, still in elementary school at the time, and the rest of the family moved to Las Vegas to join Frank. She became a true Las Vegas local, graduating from Las Vegas High School and the newly opened Nevada Southern University, later to be renamed the University of Nevada, Las Vegas (UNLV). She enjoyed a career as a Reading Specialist in the Clark County School District.

WANDERLUST

All four of my grandparents had migrated to the U.S. between 1904 and 1914. My paternal grandparents came from Lovrec', a small village that was part of the Austro-Hungarian Empire prior to World War I, then referred to as the "War to End All Wars." Lovrec' became part of Yugoslavia when it was created as part of the post-World War I settlement agreement, and after the Balkan war and in the 1990s Lovrec' became part of Croatia. My maternal grandmother came from Sisljavic, also a village in the Austro-Hungarian Empire that that became part of Yugoslavia then Croatia. My maternal grandfather was a Bosnian Serb who came from the village of Stabandza, near the Croatian border. Stabandza followed the path from being part of Austro-Hungary, then Yugoslavia, and then Bosnia.

Like so many others, I was inspired by the book "Roots," by Alex Hailey to find my relatives in then-Yugoslavia. I arranged for a one-year leave-of-absence from the school district and planned to visit Europe, then Yugoslavia. My intent was to find my roots, polish my language skills, and write the great American novel. The writing component would be done while living in the Adriatic seaside village of Novi Grad.

I had pre-paid for as much of the trip as I could and had a cache of savings that allowed my child support and other debts to continue to be paid while I was gone

Patti and I dated and I told her of my plans that would commence at the end of the summer session. Our relationship grew serious and we talked of marriage upon my return. Just before the summer session ended, Patti's mother passed away unexpectedly. Patti's father had passed away at age 50 and her mother at age 54. Patti was shattered and I was in a dilemma. My plans had been made for Europe. Should I stay home and comfort her, or continue on my trip? After much talking, crying, and wrestling with what to do I decided to go to Europe but stay in touch with Patti as often as possible.

STOPS ALONG THE WAY

Ileft Las Vegas and visited with my parents and sisters in Clairton, then went on to visit my sister Maryann and her family in Elizabethtown, Pennsylvania. From Harrisburg (near Elizabethtown) I was scheduled to fly to New York and visit Sandy, my college roommate who was married, working in the advertising business, and living in New Rochelle, New York.

While staying in Elizabethtown, Pennsylvania with my sister Maryann, I phoned Allegheny Airlines to confirm my reservation to New York, and was told I'd be flying on a DC-9, the jet model that later became the MD-80. In those days airports did not have much security, especially small airports such as the one in Harrisburg. I was to leave on an early morning flight, so I checked my duffel bag (a WW-II relic that an uncle had loaned me for the trip), and waited for the boarding call. When I looked out on the tarmac I could see two propeller planes and a DC-9. As the DC-9 began to board I walked on board and took a seat near the front of the plane.

The plane pushed back from the gate and began to move on the tarmac as the stewardess began her spiel, "Ladies and Gentlemen, welcome to Allegheny Airlines flight number such and such with service to Chicago with a stop in Pittsburgh."

I smiled, as she had obviously made a mistake. We were going to La Guardia in New York, not Chicago. I looked around the cabin and nobody seemed to have caught the goof so I said, "Ma'am, we're not going to Pittsburgh, we're going to New York."

At the time I had long hair and was dressed like a bum. She looked at me and said, "Oh my God! A hijack! This is my first flight!"

I said, "Oh, no, Ma'am" and whipped out my ticket, "I am supposed to be on a plane to New York, not Chicago."

She was still in a panic but realized at least, it was not a hijack. She went to the door that separates the cabin from the cockpit and tried to open it but it was locked. "The key... where do I put the key?" she mumbled as she reached into an area and pulled out the key, opened the cockpit door and said something to the Captain.

The plane jerked to a halt, and the Captain came back to me. He opened entry the door and a set of stairs had flipped out of the plane beneath the door—they were sometimes used in the days before jetways. He said to me, "Get out!"

And I did. The plane pulled away and I was left to walk back to the terminal. I cannot imagine such a thing happening today. It seemed as surreal then as it does now.

No employee in the terminal seemed to be particularly upset about my walking in from the tarmac. I showed my ticket and was directed to one of the propeller planes and whisked off to La Guardia Airport where my former roommate met me.

CHECKMATE IN ICELAND

The year was 1972, and American Chess Master Bobby Fischer and Russian Chess Master Boris Spassky had their famous World Chess Match in Reykjavik, Iceland. It was USSR vs. the U.S. The airline tickets I held to Europe took me on Loftleiðir Airlines, the national airline of Iceland, from New York to Luxemburg with a stopover in Iceland.

For a very reasonable fee, one could stay a few days in Iceland and be treated to tours of the area. I opted for the stay over. There were only two major hotels in Reykjavík, the Loftleiðir, which was owned by the airline, and the privately owned Saga. I stayed at the Loftleiðir, as did Bobby Fischer. Spassky was housed in the Saga. The first day I went to the hotel spa to take a swim, followed by a steam in the steam room. I'm sure very few people can say this with honesty, but I met Bobby Fischer in the nude (men are naked except for a towel while in a steam room). The stopover was well worth the extra time and cost. By the way, I cannot say that making my acquaintance inspired Bobby Fischer, but he DID win the match over the Russian champion. Of course he also became a recluse and persona non grata in the U.S. for playing a later match against Spassky in Yugoslavia, which he did despite sanctions against that country by the U.S.

THE OLD COUNTRIES

After a wonderful visit in Iceland my journey continued to Luxemburg, which was the only European port of call for Loftleiðir Airlines. The tiny country in the midst of Europe is famous for its banking. Otherwise there was not much to see, as it is one of Europe's smallest countries. The first part of my trip to Europe lived up to my expectations – traveling through thirteen countries and enjoying adventure after adventure. I sent a post card to each of my children as well as to Patti from every destination. While traveling from France to Spain I met three Canadian girls and two Australian boys on the new, state-of-the-art Spanish Talgo train, and we traveled as a group of six through Portugal. We rented a VW van and visited the seaside as well as the countryside. The cost of the rental would have been prohibitive but split six ways it was reasonable.

Soon we were back on the train and through Spain and

France when the train came to a sudden stop. As we got dis-embarked I approached an apparent railroad employee and asked if he spoke English. He nodded and I asked why the train had stopped. Another breakdown? He said no, that the union had just gone on strike and if I knew what was good for me I'd stay away from the train. We spent the night in the unheated depot on concrete benches. I wore only a heavy sweater over my clothing and it did not keep the chill out.

Nearly all train traffic had been halted in France except for a few local commuter trains. Early the following morning one such commuter train came through the village. It was so packed with people that it reminded me of pictures of trains in India, with people standing and hanging onto every small space available. The six of us forced ourselves onto the train and stood, unable to move, next to the open bathroom door for the entire 3-hour ride to Nice.

The French Riviera city of Nice was a madhouse. People were scrambling for rental cars, which were nil, and otherwise trying to book any manner of transportation. The people were wild, showing no respect for lines, nor one another. People were pushing and shoving as though it were every-man-for-himself. Somehow the six of us managed to stay together. I told my travel mates to sit tight and let me try something. Remembering my college experience in the United States as a car jockey, I went into the Hertz Car Rental office and called the manager aside. He said of course, no cars were available for rental. I asked him if he needed anything deliv-ered toward Italy and he looked at his manifest and said that he had a station wagon to be delivered to Savona, Italy. That was a perfect destination for us, and soon I pulled out of the rental lot with a station wagon, loaded up my five friends and our luggage, and we drove to Savona, Italy to deliver the car. Trains in Italy were not on strike but we parted company in Savona, as my friends headed for Rome and I headed for Trieste, the border town in Italy that served as a gateway to Yugoslavia.

Once I reached Yugoslavia, the novelty of being in the land of my heritage soon began to wear off. I had picked up a cold in the unheated train depot France, and when I reached my first Yugoslavian city, Ljubljana, I could not understand a soul, even though I thought I had at least a rudimentary grasp of the language. My grandparents spoke almost no English and my parents used both languages in the home. I did not realize that the dialect in the Slovenian part of Yugoslavia was different from Croatian, and was therefore difficult to understand. Sick, frustrated, and depressed, I found a phone and called Patti to see how she was doing, and then I called my parents. The phone call to my parents went as follows (remember, I was 29 years old at the time and have not lived at home since I was 17):

Me: "Hi Mom"

Mother: "You don't sound good."

ME: "I caught a cold in France."

Mother: "I knew it. You didn't take your winter coat."

ME: "Mom, I have a very heavy sweater. It is fine."

Mother: "No, you need a coat. Where do you go next?"

ME: "I'll be in Zagreb tomorrow, why?"

Mother: "I'm sending your father over with your winter coat. You left it here with us."

ME: "No, Mom, really... I'll buy a coat. I promise."

Mother: "No, I know you, you're too cheap. Go to the Continental Hotel in Zagreb. Your father will meet you there."

ME: "No, Mom, really..."

Mother: "He'll be there in the morning. Love you." Click.

There was method to her madness. My father and I had never been close. My parents had traveled to Yugoslavia over 22 consecutive summers, spoke like natives, and knew the country intimately. She thought it would be a good bonding experience for both of us. Even though they had just returned a few weeks earlier, she put my father on a plane and off he went. The next morning I walked into the Continental Hotel in Zagreb and there in the lobby, on an overstuffed couch, sat my father. We spent a week together riding the bus to villages that he'd recently left, and meeting relatives. In one particular village, the relative who answered the door was so stunned to see my father so soon after he'd gone, he blessed himself and asked, "Did somebody die?"

During our week together my mother's plan did not work as she had hoped. Although the country of Yugoslavia was made up of seven or so former countries, it was small by American standards, each country being more like the size of a county in the U.S. The entire country of Yugoslavia was the size of the state of New Jersey. We visited the village of my grandparent's birth as well as many others. My father pointed out which families had left each particular village to migrate to Clairton. We did indeed get to meet many of the relatives but throughout the trip his mantra was, "You need to get back home and marry that girl. We've talked to her on the phone. She has a good heart. Quit all this foolishness and get back to work like a normal person." And so it went. After he returned home, I did begin to become concerned that Patti might be having a difficult time of it so I cut my trip short and in early December returned to Las Vegas.

SECOND TRY GOT IT RIGHT

Shortly before Patti's Christmas holiday from the school district began I popped the question and she said yes. We married in a small ceremony on December 15, 1972 and planned to drive to her sister's house in Orange County, leave my car there, and fly to Hawaii on our honeymoon. The day before the wedding Patti had dental work scheduled and while she was numb the dentist suggested he take her wisdom teeth out so they did not cause her future problems in the. She agreed and the following day, when we married, she looked like a chipmunk and was on heavy medication.

We went to the courthouse for an informal ceremony. Dave and Margi Hoff, Patti's friends from the school district, stood up as witnesses. The trip to Orange County, where her sister had wedding cake and a small party, as well as the flight to Hawaii, was miserable for Patti as the effects of the Novocain wore off.

We flew directly to Hawaii, the Big Island, as I wanted something quaint. However, Patti was expecting something from the Hawaii brochures. That was our first miscommunication. The first night we went to a small restaurant inside the home of a local family. It was all very Hawaiian. A little urchin peeked around the oilcloth that was positioned between the kitchen and the small dining area. It was a miserable introduction for Patti to Hawaii as well as to marriage. I felt so bad for her.

The next day we flew to Waikiki and stayed there for the balance of the honeymoon. We took the city bus to the Ala Maona Shopping Center and did some sightseeing. On the return trip to our hotel, an older gentleman on the bus struck up a conversation with us. He was a real gentleman who looked like he was homeless and when I insisted on paying his fare he did not object. He got off at the Ili Kai, a very exclusive hotel in Waikiki. As the bus started to move the driver laughed and said, "He did it again." I looked confused and he added, "The man rides the bus every day, pretends to be a pauper, strikes up a conversation, and usually gets a tourist to feel sorry for him pay his fare. He owns that hotel."

We both had a good laugh and things started getting better for Patti. Her swelling had gone down, the pain was gone, we were staying in a real hotel, and an NFL playoff game was about to begin (Patti is a rabid football fan). I was also interested because the Steelers were playing. We watched the playoff game on a black-and-white TV with rabbit ears antenna and a snowy picture as Franco Harris made the so-called "immaculate reception." and the Steelers won the game. That was our first and only Christmas in Hawaii.

A NEW MARRIAGE WITH
LIMO SERVICE

Patti and I had married in mid-December. However, since my school district leave of absence was still in effect, I drove limo, and planned to do so the rest of the school year. During the previous summer, taxis in Las Vegas had gone on strike and the only means of transport was limo service. Jim Bell added as many limousines to his fleet as he was able to find, and asked me if I knew of any teachers who might want to drive limo for the summer. I contacted several, including longtime friend and teacher Don Creekmore, as well as another friend, Chuck Garhardt. The strike ended but several teachers continued to drive part time including Don, who was expecting a new baby and needed the extra money. After my honeymoon had ended, I was driving full time and Don continued to drive part time. Don had picked up a fare at the airport one Sunday and the man had chartered his limo for the balance of his trip.

It is not unusual for a man who comes to Las Vegas alone to hire a taxi or limousine driver for an extended period of time while in Vegas. It is a male bonding need I suspect, but the patron will often ask the driver to accompany him as he gambles, attends shows, and such. The driver serves as a personal valet of sorts.

As Don relates the story, the gentleman, who was pretty well inebriated when he entered the limo, was one of several people who opted to take the airport limousine to their various hotels. This particular fare was the last to enter and sat in the front seat as the rest of the limo was occupied. After depositing the other riders at their respective hotels, Don headed to the Sands to drop off the last customer. As Don continued his drive from the airport, the man in question laid a $20 bill on the seat next to him and said, "I would like to have your attention." Don nodded and the man laid another 20 on the seat and the man asked, "Do I have your attention?"

Don said, "Yes Sir," and continued to drive. The man laid one more 20 on the seat and asked, "Do I have your UNDIVIDED attention?"

Don replied, "Absolutely," and the man said he would like to charter this limousine for an undetermined amount of time.

Don took the gentleman, who identified himself as "Mr. Pike" to the Sands, where his room was "comped" (provided at no charge—complimentary) and clearly treated as a "whale," meaning he was given all the amenities of the hotel free of charge because he was a major gambler. When Mr. Pike told the personnel at the Sands that Don was his personal driver they were a little miffed, as they would have preferred to use their own company limousine and keep Mr. Pike at their property as long as possible. But he made it clear that he had his own driver so after getting his room, doing a little gambling, and being fawned over by the staff, he and Don set out to some casino hopping. The Sands Security detail insisted one of their security guards goes along. Mr. Pike agreed. He loved the attention.

They continued their Vegas venture well into the night, but Don had to teach school the following day, so after several hours he called in to his dispatcher and explained his dilemma. The dispatcher phoned me at home to ask if I could take the balance of the charter and I said of course. I drove to the Hilton and Don took my car back to the company garage where he left it and picked up his own. The client was so drunk he did not realize there'd been a change in drivers.

Don gave me a brief summary of what had happened up to that point, but I could not have imagined that this would become perhaps my most memorable night of driving limo, if not one of the most profitable. Don told me that the gentleman had "taken very good care of me so far…" code for the fact that he was a very good tipper.

The mystery man went by the name of Mr. Claude Pike (although I'm sure that was not his real name) of New Orleans (which was probably not his real place of residence). I became Mr. Pike's driver at the Las Vegas Hilton Hotel after Don and I switched places. I had been a private chauffer on other occasions, but this one would top them all.

Mr. Pike had taken a marker for $20,000 at the Hilton and was just about at the end of his funds on that marker. A marker is an IOU that a gambler provides in exchange for cash or chips with which to gamble. Don told me he had taken several markers at other hotels including $30,000 at the Sands, where he was staying.

When his money from the marker had run out at the Hilton he decided to go back to the Sands. By that time he had taken markers of at least $60,000 by my count. At the Sands he took another $30,000 marker and proceeded to run through it in short order, playing mostly at the craps table. He turned to me and said, "Let's try our luck at another hotel," over the pleas of the boxmen and other Sands officials. Once they saw he was going to leave the property they again sent a uniformed security guard to accompany him. He decided to go to the Stardust and the three of us walked into the casino.

As he had done at the other hotels, the Sands security guard tried to be invisible, which was difficult in his khaki Sands uniform at the Stardust, whose security guards wore blue uniforms. I could see the disdain on the faces of the Stardust officials but they did nothing for the moment.

Mr. Pike headed for the Cashier's cage with me next to him. He said to the cashier, in his Southern accent, "Ah want some money."

The cashier, a balding fellow who looked like an accountant, was polite and asked, "Do you have credit with us, Sir?"

Mr. Pike said, "I ain't got nothin. I want some gamblin' money."

The cashier, still straight and professional then asked, "Would you fill out this credit application for me?"

I could see Mr. Pike was both irritated and in a devilish mood and answered the cashier with, "I ain't fillin' out nothin. I want some gamblin' money."

This back-and-forth went on for several minutes until somebody apparently recognized him as a whale (high roller) and called the cage. A young woman in the cage took the call and soon came to the window to relieve the cashier who had been helping Mr. Pike. With a smile that was dripping sugar and an accent just as thick as his, she said, "Hi there, would y'all like some money?"

Mr. Pike smiled and sheepishly said, "Yeah."

She said, "How much y'all want?"

"Uhh, I dunno. Maybe 'bout 20."

"Y'all got a driver's license?"

"Yeah."

"Tell ya what, y'all show me yer driver's license and I'll git $20,000 fer ya. How's that?"

"Fine."

With that she glanced at his license, had him sign a note, and gave him $20K.

After he had gambled a few thousand dollars Mr. Pike caught sight of a small scuffle of sorts out of the corner of his eye. He said, "What's the problem?" and one of the hotel officials said that the uniformed Sands security guard would have to leave. Company policy did not permit a security guard in uniform from another hotel to be on site without prior arrangement.

Mr. Pike gathered up the remainder of his chips and said, "Let's go."

Once the Stardust suits realized they were about to lose a whale, they said, "Oh, he can stay." But it was too late. Mr. Pike was headed for the cage to cash in. The young lady who had given him the marker was gone so he asked the male cashier his name. The male cashier told him it was Jim and he handed all his chips to Jim and said, "Y'all put this in an envelope fer that little lady." I'm sure she was stunned when she came to work the next night and discovered she'd been left about an $18,000 tip.

From there we again went to the Hilton where he breezed through another $20,000 marker, making his running losses at least $100,000 that I knew of. But the night was not over.

Several times during the evening he said to me, "Son, I like you. You remind me of my own son," as he handed me a black ($100) chip. Before the night was over I had accumulated 8 or 9 black chips plus additional chips from bets he'd placed for me using his money. On one occasion he said, "You know, my son wanted to go to Duke University to be a doctor but he was dumb as a post and got rejected three times. Finally I donated two and a half million for a building on campus. My son is a doctor today with a degree from Duke."

We left the Hilton and returned to the Sands. Keep in mind that Mr. Pike had been very generous with everybody;

spreading black chips around like they were $1 chips. After an hour or so on the tables he moved to the bar and within a few minutes his face plopped down on the bar as he passed out, drunk. The bartenders and security guards rushed to his side, wiped his face, and brought him around and he said he might want to go to his room and rest for a while. The head security guard caught my eye and pointed to the door, signaling me to leave, which I did not want to do. Pretending to not see the head security guard, I asked Mr. Pike if he wanted me to leave. He said no, that he was going to lie down for a while and for me to come up to his tower suite and wait.

I had never been in the Sands Tower before where the suites rented for thousands of dollars per night but were all comped. Mr. Pike and I and three security guards trekked toward the suite as he said to me, "Order whatever you want. It is all comped. Get yourself the best steak in the house and a half dozen bottles of Johnny Walker Red Label to take home with you. Don't worry, it's all on me." (Note: Neither the Sands nor the Sands Tower exist today. They were demolished and the Venetian Hotel were built in their place. However, the Convention Center at the Venetian Hotel still uses the Sands name).

By this time it was about 2:30 or 3:00 a.m. I immediately called Patti from the room and said, "Guess where I am!" and started to tell her when she said, from her deep slumber, "Why don't you tell me about it tomorrow?"

Mr. Pike was still a little unsteady on his feet and the

security guards had helped him into the bedroom and were undressing him to put him to bed when he called out to me, "I'll just take a short nap. We'll go out again so stay where you are. Order something from Room Service"

I looked toward the bedroom and there was a full-length mirror that was angled so I was able to see all four people in the bedroom suite. They had placed Mr. Pike on the bed and as he drifted off to sleep were... ROBBING HIM! They were cleaning out his pockets of the thousands of dollars in chips and filling their own pockets. I sat stunned. First, they were security guards who were supposed to watch over him, not rob him! Second, Mr. Pike had been most generous to all employees including the security guards, and had already tipped them thousands. But the greedy bastards were taking more. They finally left and gave me a threatening stare as if to say, "Keep your mouth shut if you know what's good for you."

About 30 minutes later while I was enjoying my steak and lobster with a coke and two bottles of Johnny Walker Red Label by my side to take home, there came a knock on the door. The most stunning blonde I had ever seen was standing in the doorway, dressed to kill. She said to me, "Hi, are you Mr. Pike?"

I stood frozen for several seconds then responded with, " Are you a hooker?"

She smiled again and said, "I'm anything you want me to be, Honey."

I proceeded to tell her that Mr. Pike was taking a little nap and did not want to be disturbed as he was going to go out and gamble in a little while. What a bumpkin! She said, "Well, let me see about that," and she brushed past me into the bedroom. A few minutes later Mr. Pike emerged from the bedroom and said, "Change of plans, Son. You can take some time off but be here at six sharp to take me to the airport. Do not be one minute late."

I told him I would be there and went home to freshen up, taking my booty with me. When I returned at a few minutes before six there stood Mr. Pike in a professional business suit and looking fresh as a daisy. I had been well rewarded for my company and loyalty the previous night. When I got home I counted up the chips he had given me, including the spoils from the bets he would occasionally lay down for me; it totaled well over $1,200. Not bad for a night's work. We put his luggage into the limo and I headed for the private side of the airport. He settled his limousine bill with cash, then gave me a couple of 20s for a tip. That tip alone, not counting the previous night, was one of the largest single tips I'd ever received. But after having been spoiled by the big bucks from the previous evening, my first reaction was, "What a cheapskate." He was not nearly as generous sober as he had been drunk. Still, on second thought, there I was, complaining in my mind about my second biggest tip ever! What an idiot I was.

On the way to the plane, (he was taking a private Lear Jet home, probably compliments of the Sands) Mr. Pike let me know that Pike was not his real name and that I had never seen him in Las Vegas, and if I ever did see him I did not know or recognize him. He then softened a bit and said that he did appreciate my loyalty from the previous night and said he would answer any one question as long as it did not compromise his personal security. I thought for a minute and asked, "What do you own?"

Without a blink he responded, "Son, I own five state governors." We pulled up to the plane, and I loaded the luggage onto the Lear Jet. He smiled, shook my hand and got on the plane. I never again saw or spoke to him but have kept the thoughts of that evening as a chauffeur to a high roller prominent in my memory bank.

BACK TO EDUCATION

Besides the action Mr. Pike had provided, the limo business in December and January was pretty dead. I was, for the most part, an unemployed married man living off my savings and Patti's generosity. My leave of absence from the school district was in effect for the rest of the school year. I decided to give substitute teaching a try since I was not under contract. Substitute teaching, I soon discovered, was nothing like having one's own regular classroom. As a sub you did not know your students nor were you sensitive to any special needs they might have. A sub would usually just see students for a day or two and the kids saw this time as vacation time away from the regular drudgery of their classroom teacher. It was interesting, however, as my first assignment was at an inner city junior high school populated by mostly Hispanic children of non or limited English-speaking parents. As I walked into the classroom I heard plenty of chatter in Spanish. The chatter continued as I wrote my name on the board, took out the notes left by the regular teacher, and began to tell the class – in Spanish – that we were going to have the exact same lesson that the regular teacher would have normally been there. Once I began speaking in Spanish the class became hushed. A student called out, "Are you Mexican?"

I did not answer directly but told them I also speak some Japanese, then asked, "Does that make me Japanese?" I spent the first few minutes talking about the advantage of young people who could speak more than one language and encouraged them to become proficient in as many languages as possible as that would help them get a good job. The class was very quiet and after they left the word must have gotten around because I had no problems the rest of the day.

The Clark County School District, which includes Las Vegas, has a policy of naming elementary schools after educators, junior high and middle schools after pioneers, and high schools after geographical landmarks. James Cashman was a Las Vegas pioneer but also the owner of the local Cadillac dealership. Many joked that the school named in his honor was named for the Cadillac dealership.

My second or third teaching assignment was at James Cashman Junior High School, and to my surprise my former elementary school kids from my first year in Las Vegas at Rex Bell were now ninth grade students at Cashman, so although I was a sub, many of the students knew me. The day went very well.

As I was returning my keys and preparing to leave school at the end of the day, the secretary asked if I could wait because the principal wanted to speak to me. Principal Richard Priest had come from Iowa where he had been a teacher and principal. He was a laid back Middle American with heartland values and was an excellent administrator. He told me that he had observed my interaction with the students and asked if I would consider a permanent sub position for the rest of the year. Ironically he had been a friend in Iowa of Las Vegas principal Galen Good, the principal who hired me to teach at Rex Bell. In fact they signed their contracts to come to Las Vegas at the same time and their families had driven cross-country together.

Mr. Priest went on to say that there was a class of 12 boys who had been the bane of their teacher, causing said teacher to take a medical leave, and that the 12 boys had already run off several other subs. Some teachers referred to the group as "The Dirty Dozen." Mr. Priest said he had contacted the other two principals for whom I had worked and both said I had excellent classroom management skills. He then asked again if I would become a permanent sub.

I told Mr. Priest that I was flattered by his offer but I was unwilling to return to work fulltime as a substitute. Substitute teachers earn a fraction of the salaries of contracted teachers and have no benefits, although permanent subs earn a higher salary than regular ones. He said that if I would do this favor for him he would do whatever he could to have my contract reinstated early. He said the Dirty Dozen would be redistributed to other classes at the end of the semester – a few weeks away, and he just needed somebody to keep the lid on things until then. I gave him until the end of the semester to get my contract reinstated and he agreed. I agreed to become a permanent sub until then. Within a week my contract had been reinstated.

The Dirty Dozen proved to be no problem for me. None were stupid, and several were fairly bright. They were, for the most part, just junior high boys without a father figure in the home and were testing the limits. We got along well and I told them that if everybody kept up their grades, had minimal discipline referrals, and good attendance for the rest of the term that I would reward them. They asked "With what?" And I took that moment to brainstorm with them. Their wish was to take a camping trip into the wilds of Nevada.

I took the idea to Mr. Priest and he loved it. He said he had a fund that would pay for the rental of a camper, and the trip would be educational as the class I taught was a science class. We used the rest of the time to design the camping trip – a class project to identify the flora and fauna of the region. All the boys brought their signed parental permission slips within a day. We sent the itinerary home for the boys to give to their parents. The trip took place on a weekend so I took Steve Rudish, my cousin and a Physical Education teacher, as a second chaperone. Steve had done lots of camping and my own experience in that field was limited.

SATURDAY MORNING DEPARTURE

I pulled up in the camper at 6:30 a.m. for the 7:00 a.m. sendoff. All the boys were there a half hour early and several parents thanked me profusely. One mother called me aside and attempted to hand me a $100 bill saying that according to the itinerary we were going past the Chicken Ranch, a brothel where she had worked for years. She said, "I want you to use this money to get my son laid."

I thought, "Am I on Candid Camera?" But she was sincere. I told her I could not do that and she tried once more, promising me it would be just between us. I graciously declined.

As we drove up the highway the boys began to go into the rest room at the rear of the camper one at a time. I could smell the Marijuana wafting through the vehicle but was not sure how I was going to deal with it. By lunchtime we were in a ghost town where we stopped to have a picnic. It was warm outside and the boys left their coats inside the vehicle. Steve was getting things set up when I returned to the camper on the pretext of using the rest room. Once inside I went through all their coat pockets and confiscated their stashes of Marijuana.

After lunch as we drove along, I quietly held one hand out the window and dropped one baggie at a time onto the highway. Nobody missed the pot until we pulled onto a side road to camp for the night. I could hear hushed conversations:

"Where is the stuff? You were supposed to bring it."

"I DID!"

"Well, where is it?"

"Maybe it fell out. Let's look."

I asked innocently, "What's the problem, fellas?"

"Oh, nothing."

They never figured it out. They blamed each other for a while then just chalked it up to one of life's mysteries. The rest of the trip was uneventful except for Steve's scare stories about axe murders in the desert. The semester ended and the boys were redistributed.

CAN'T SPELL
ADMINISTRATOR NOW I
ACCIDENTLY ARE ONE

A couple of weeks after my contract had been reinstated I got a call at home from Principal Dick Priest. He asked if I would be willing to be the Dean of Students effective Monday. The school was built for a maximum of 1,100 but housed more than 1,500 students. That was enough to merit two Dean positions. One Dean, Arnold Addington, was an older heavy-drinking ex-Marine and Okie who looked a bit like Mr. Clean. He took no sass and gave no quarter. The other was a tall young Mormon man from rural Nevada. The inner city kids, who made up about a third of the school population, knew exactly how to pull his strings. He was having a very difficult year. He was the chaperone for a Valentines Day dance and had apparently ejected a couple of kids whom retaliated by vandalizing his truck. That was the last straw. He quit on the spot and moved back to rural Nevada and away from the inner city population. I agreed to replace him and, just as I had begun a career in education with little training or experience, so did I venture into Education Administration.

Typically, a school administrator has no classroom duties but I asked Dick if I could continue to teach at least one course. Since my administrative duties would include Discipline and Attendance issues, my logic was that I could better keep my fingers on the pulse of the student body if I were still teaching. Dick was a very innovative principal and he liked the idea. He told me that the school district had selected several schools, including Cashman, to pilot a program for Gifted Child Education. Since there was not yet a designated teacher for that class, that could be my teaching assignment. It worked out perfectly.

THE ACCIDENTAL
DOCTORAL STUDENT

By this time I had completed my Master's degree in Educational Psychology from Northern Arizona University in Flagstaff, and had taken additional courses in Educational Administration at UNLV. My favorite professor at UNLV, Jack Dettre, was in the midst of designing the school's first Doctoral program. I applied for the program and was accepted into the initial class. However, since I had only been an administrator for a few weeks, I did not believe I had the political connections to get into the Educational Administration track. Active principals and District Office administrators immediately grabbed most of those slots. I had no coursework, background or experience in Special Education, so that area was out. The only other major area of study, and the one I chose by default was Secondary Education/Curriculum and Instruction. There were only two students who had been accepted into that major, and since the program was so new, I was allowed plenty of flexibility to design my program. I asked my committee if I could specialize in Gifted Child Education and my committee members said, "Bring us a proposal."

In the process of doing research to design a proposal that included a course of study I discovered that there were practically no universities offering a specialization in that field. I contacted experts in the field (those who had written extensively). That research resulted in my building a close friendship with one of the premier authorities in the field – Dr. Joseph Renzulli of the University of Connecticut. He referred me to Dr. Dorothy Sisk of the University of South Florida, who had just accepted a position within the U.S. Department of Education that oversaw Gifted Child Education. It was a new and exciting field and I was on the cutting edge. The committee accepted my proposal.

The other doctoral student in Secondary Education/ Curriculum and Instruction was a 52-year-old Spanish teacher from Las Vegas High School, Patti's alma mater. Ramona Gustin, whose husband Charles was the general manager of the Dunes Hotel, and lived on site, was my only classmate.

That summer, Dick Priest was transferred to Brinley Junior High School and took me with him as Dean of Students. Brinley was located in the far Northwest part of Las Vegas, which was then on the outskirts of town. As a bonus I was able to start a Gifted Ed program at that school to support my Doctoral studies.

The following year, as my doctoral program became more intense, and I needed to be closer to UNLV for meetings and such. I took a position at Orr Jr. High School, less than a mile from the UNLV campus. The principal, another ex-pat Pittsburgh area guy and Slippery Rock University alumnus, was Frank Lamping. He was very understanding in allowing me to leave campus to attend meetings at UNLV. In return I helped him establish an extra position at the school. Frank, like Dick Priest, was a most innovative administrator. He discovered that I had a minor and a teaching endorsement in Library Science. His librarian retired from the school district just before the year began so he wrote me officially as the librarian. He then hired a para-professional (non-degreed) clerical person to be my full time library aid, which freed me to become an off-the-books administrative assistant to the principal and help with the duties of the Dean. I would come to school early and my aide and I would go over the requirements for the library for the day. She would conduct the daily library business and I would move to my Office of the Dean of Students. Two birds. One stone.

My Doctoral degree was granted in 1978. It might also be noted that both principals, Frank Lamping and Richard Priest as well as the late John Vandenberg, who was a vice-principal during my tenure at Orr, have since had schools named in their honor.

Orr Junior High School drew from homes on the Desert Inn golf course. One student was repeatedly sent to my office for minor infractions such as not having a pencil, not doing his homework, not paying attention, and the like. I sent him home one day with a form for a Required Parent Conference.

The student was the son of Chicago mob enforcer Tony "The Ant" Spilotro. (Joe Pesci played his character in the movie "Casino"). Mr. Spilotro showed up for the conference with his girlfriend, (the Sharon Stone character in the movie), and his son. I explained very carefully the issue with his son, that he was not a problem kid, but the things he was not doing were preventing him from getting a good education.

Mr. Splitro looked at his son and asked, "Is that man telling me right?" The lad, with tears in his eyes, nodded his assent. Then, BAM! Spilotro reached over and slapped the kid hard across the face and said, "You listen to this man. I want you to get an education so you don't end up like me. Capice?"

The son nodded and Tony thanked me for taking the time with his son and said to call him anytime. Then he added, "You come down the Gold Bug and pick out something nice for your wife. Anything you want. And you let me know if you EVER have any trouble."

I thanked him and walked the couple to the door and shook hands. The Gold Bug was a jewelry store on Sahara Avenue. I was savvy enough to know that was where his gang, dubbed "The Hole in the Wall Gang," for blasting through the roofs or walls of upscale jewelry stores, fenced their stolen goods. Of course I never did take him up on his offer but the teachers razzed me about the parent conference, suggesting I start my car by remote control.

DR. FORGOT IS BORN

At some point in my Doctoral studies Dr. Joe Renzulli was the keynote speaker at a conference in Lake Tahoe. The topic was Gifted Child Education, which was the major focus of my course of study, so I also arranged to make a minor presentation at the conference. I was very excited and had thoroughly researched, written and rewritten my presentation.

The conference was to begin on a Sunday and I scheduled a flight to Reno for 8:00 that morning. I had taken my notes home for the weekend to practice and when I completed my mock presentation for the umpteenth time, I placed my notes in my briefcase and placed it in the back seat of the car. I wanted to give myself time to forget about the presentation to clear my head. I would have time to do a final review once I arrived in Tahoe.

Saturday morning I glanced in my briefcase and somehow

missed some of my notes. I did not see them and immediately phoned the vice principal, John Vandenberg, and said "I think I locked my notes in my office at school. Can I come by and pick up your key? I'll grab my notes on the way to the airport Sunday morning and lock your keys in your office."

He said, "Fine," and I went to his house and picked up the keys to the school. I was comfortable with my presentation but wanted the backup of my notes just in case I went blank or was asked a question that needed a double check.

Sunday morning bright and early Patti and I had breakfast and she pulled on a robe over her nightclothes. She would drive me to the school, which was on the way to the airport, and I would pick up my notes.

Orr Junior High School was built in an odd architectural fashion. The office area was in one large pod and classrooms were built in spoke-like fashion adjacent to the administrative pod. The Little Theater was located on the edge of the administrative pod and the only door that was not chained from the inside was the side entry to the Little Theater. I entered through that door, walked the length of the theater and out the main entry into the administrative pod. The doors closed behind me, of course. I looked through my office and did not find my notes. Turns out they were in my briefcase the entire time and I had simply overlooked them. Duh! I chuckled to myself and unlocked the office complex, placed the key on John Vandenberg's desk, and exited the office complex. The door locked behind me and I reversed my trail for my exit, but as I tried to open the door to the

Little Theater I realized it was locked, and I had just locked the master key in the vice-principal's office. All the outside doors were chained from the inside and I had no keys to unlock them. I was locked inside the school!!

Patti was sitting in the car in her robe listening to the radio as I pounded on the doors and windows to get her attention. Finally she heard me and came to the door where I shouted, "I'm locked in! Can you go to Frank Lamping's house to get his master keys?"

Frank, the principal, lived close by. We had been to his house together on one occasion and I had been driving. Patti said she thought she could find his house so at 7:00 a.m. on a Sunday morning, dressed in a robe and nightclothes, she went driving through the neighborhood where he lived. The first two joggers she asked did not know Frank but the third did and directed Patti to his house. Patti, still in her robe of course, sans makeup, and with her hair in disarray, rang the bell. Frank's wife, Betty Lou, answered the door. When Patti asked if Frank was home, Betty Lou turned and said icily, "FRANK! There is a woman at the door for you."

Patti got the keys, sprung me from my captivity in the school, and we raced to the airport, breaking every possible speed law en route. Fortunately, the Highway Patrol must have been having coffee and donuts that morning because we were not stopped. I did not bother to check in at the airport, but instead ran as fast as I could and arrived at the gate for the Hughes Airwest flight to Reno just as they were closing the jet-way door. They let me board and since there were only about a half dozen other passengers on the flight my carry-on luggage presented no problem. I collapsed and eventually made it to the conference.

Dr. Joseph Renzulli from the University of Connecticut was, and still is, an icon in the field of Gifted Child Education. He had written and researched more than anybody else in the field. His keynote presentation was most enlightening, and he attended my presentation, which went well. We met at the bar that evening and talked until the sun came up the following morning. The result was a long lasting personal and professional friendship that exists to this day, more than three decades later.

At the urging of John Vandenberg, Vice Principal and practical-joker-in-chief at Orr Junior High School, the staff had redecorated my office with renderings of an absent-minded professor. Additionally, the room was filled with posters that announced, "WELCOME HOME DR. FORGOT." From that day forward my nickname has been Dr. Forgot.

MOVING TOWARD DOCTOR STATUS

The Doctoral program was fun for the most part. It required lots of writing, which suited me just fine. My fellow student in the program did not really want a Doctorate for career advancement, as she was just a few years from retirement (available at age 55 in Clark County School District). She wanted it for the status. Her husband Charles was General Manager of the Dunes Hotel and Casino, a premier hotel property on the Strip. Its "Top of the Dunes Restaurant" was one of the most elegant on the Strip. But even more elegant was another Dunes restaurant, "Dome of the Sea," that included a harp-playing mermaid who sat on a pedestal in a pool and played for the customer's enjoyment. The Dunes also had Sasha's strolling violins, gorgeous young ladies who did exactly what the name implied. One of my high school students from Western, Stephanie Skandros, was a member of the strolling violins for years. Stephanie's mother was the school secretary at my wife Patti's school. Just another example of why Las Vegans referred to their hometown as, "Big city. Small town."

Charles Gustin was required to live on the property due to the nature of his job so he and Ramona lived a lifestyle quite different from any I had known. All their meals were either taken in one of the restaurants or delivered to the suite in which they lived.

Behind the hotel, nestled between the property and Interstate Highway-15, was the Dunes golf course and a huge Sultan that welcomed Las Vegas visitors who passed.

The Dunes no longer exists. It was purchased by Steve Wynn and torn down then blown up, in an international TV display of an orgy of fireworks. The golf course disappeared and became part of the new property—Bellagio.

Ramona was a very good student but had not been in an intense academic program for many years and about midway through the program she phoned me and said she was dropping out. A project that was due had simply overwhelmed her. I told her that she was too far into the program to drop out and if she did so I would not have anybody to go through the rest of the program with. I then offered to help her on the project and she accepted. That weekend I went to their suite, a penthouse at the top of the Dunes, and we worked nearly 24 hours straight. All food was catered and Charles had arranged for a room for me in the event I wanted to nap (I didn't). By Sunday morning the project had been completed. Ramona was still in the program, and I had gotten one more glimpse of how the other half lives.

I am not sure if Ramona ever graduated but it was no picnic doing a Doctoral program while working full time. During that time I was not working a second job so my high energy level suited me well to work on the Doctorate.

Once the course work was completed, it was time to start on my Dissertation. Somebody told me that the longer the title on one's Dissertation the less scrutiny it would receive, so my Dissertation title became, "A Comparative Analysis of the Curricular Characteristics Recommended in the Writings of Twelve Authorities in the Field of Gifted Child Education Versus Curricular Characteristics Found in Programs of Gifted Child Education Programs of All United State's School Districts with a Student Population in Excess of 10,000 Children."

Because the initial Doctoral Program at the University of Nevada, Las Vegas was too new to be accredited on its own; the Program received initial accreditation under the longer-established University of Nevada, Reno (UNR). It was written up to be a University of Nevada degree. Thus, each student in the Program at UNLV was required to spend two semesters at UNR and vice versa. We were permitted to attend the semesters during consecutive summers.

The first summer I rented a house in Reno. A schoolteacher who was gone in the summer owned the house. Patti came up occasionally but for the most part she stayed in Las Vegas. Her birthday is in late June and she had come up the week prior so we could celebrate together. I decided to surprise her with a Datsun 260-Z sports car for her birthday.

I arranged everything by phone and had one of our friends, an art teacher, make a big blue bow and place it atop the car in our garage, while Patti spent her birthday week with me in Reno. When it was time for her to return to Las Vegas, I told her I had an early meeting so one of the other Doc students, who was in on the surprise, agreed to drive her to the airport for her Friday morning flight.

In fact I left on an earlier flight so when she landed in Las Vegas and went to gather her bag, I walked up behind her and gave her a big birthday kiss. She was really surprised and happy that we would be spending her birthday weekend at home. When we approached the house I told her that the battery in the garage door opener seemed to be malfunctioning and that she needed to walk up close to the door to open it, which she did, revealing her birthday present – a Silver-blue Datsun 260-Z sports car!

The car was gorgeous but the 260Z was notorious for engine problems. It turned out to be a lemon and we traded it in less than a year. But it was a great surprise.

Because the Doctoral program was the first ever at UNLV, the campus library was sorely lacking as a research library. I was simply unable to do the dissertation level research I needed at that library. This problem was solved with the help of other universities. At the end of my summer semester at UNR, we drove home via the California Coastal route, stopping at every major university library; Stanford, University of California, Berkley, University of San Francisco, University of Pacific, then down to University of California, Los

Angeles (UCLA), and University of Southern California. The best option was one of the UCLA libraries, as they had one dedicated to just Graduate Education and for $50 per semester and my UNLV ID, I was granted full library privileges. They had an excellent Ph.D. Program in Education and hundreds of Doctoral Dissertations were available. Most of my research was done at that library.

During the year of writing of my dissertation my routine would be as follows: I would take the first flight out on Saturday morning to Los Angeles, rent a car and drive to Westwood and the UCLA Graduate Education Library, hole up in the library until it was about to close, load up on books that would last me two weeks, return my car and take the last flight home. I did that every other week while I wrote the dissertation.

PAGING DR. NIXON?

Finally the dissertation was completed and the only thing left to do before being awarded the degree was a Dissertation Defense. Bob McCord was going through the Educational Administration Doctoral program at the same time I was in the Curriculum and Instruction program, and we both worked at the same school. His defense was scheduled two weeks before mine. I was anxious for him but he said he was in and out in 45 minutes. So I figured, "Great! A mere formality." I couldn't have been more wrong!

The defender, that would be me, is brought into a room that is set up like a Star Chamber Inquisition. One of my committee members, who had been the most difficult on me during the entire degree program, was first up with a question. Fortunately, he was not the Chair, but he did ask the first question which went as follows, "Why did you use that particular statistical treatment with your data?"

Easy one, I thought, and began to justify my use of the particular statistical treatment. I had taken a Psychological Statistics course as a Psychology major while at BYU. The text used in that class was a classic in the field and I had used it again as the basis of my statistical treatment for my dissertation. In the entire book, there were only 12-15 pages that spoke to the treatment I had used. I was clueless about the rest of the book but I knew those 12-15 pages by heart. So when Dr. Krank (not his real name), my antagonist, asked my why I had used that treatment, I told him it was taken from the classic Statistics book. He said he was intimately familiar with the text and that page 213 specifically states that the treatment I had used was inappropriate for my type of data.

I was on a roll and responded, "You are absolutely correct Professor, but if you thumb forward to pages 221-223 you will find the list of exceptions that allows for that treatment on my type of data. I used the third exception"

He did not ask another question and I thought I was about finished. Wrong again! The rest of the committee began with rapid-fire questions – difficult ones. The ordeal went on for 2 ½ hours at which point I was physically, mentally, and emotionally drained. It had been a long three years trying to balance a high stress administrative job and a doctoral program and write a dissertation. I was worn out and this ordeal became my tipping point. I stood up and said, "Gentlemen, I have nothing more to give. Pass me if you want. Fail me if you choose. I don't care. I am finished. This meeting has just concluded." I picked up my briefcase and staggered out of the room and was halfway down the hall when my Committee Chair caught up to me. He said, "What the Hell are you trying to pull?" I said, "Nothing. I was as honest as I could be. I don't care. I have nothing left to give."

He smiled, and said, "Oh, Hell, Congratulations, Doctor. You passed. We decided before you arrived that it was our job to make you sweat. We knew you'd ace the Defense and the only one who had doubts was Professor Krank, whom you took care of after one question. Come on back in so the committee can congratulate you properly.

I guess I never was much good at initiation rites. I didn't like it, and although they all hugged me, congratulated me, and called me Doctor, all my fears of being stupid, failing courses, and not being able to live up to academic standards rushed through me. One more time, Academia became Wacademia in my mind. What should have been a happy experience was a hollow almost bitter one. But, hey, I got over it.

AN ASIAN INTERLUDE

When I left Western High School for my trip to Europe the principal who had hired me to teach Psychology was also leaving. Nils Bayless would open the new Eldorado High School on the East side of town. The incoming principal was Dr. Bruce Miller. I never did work for him but we went through the Doctoral program at the same time and became friends. Bruce was a mover and shaker in various national organizations devoted to Educational Administration. One such organization was AAPHER, the national association for teachers of Health, Physical Education and Recreation. They were planning to invite the international organization, ICHPER to meet in Las Vegas with the U.S. organization. Bruce was on the committee to try to get ICHPER to come to Las Vegas, and because I was writing a newspaper column at the time he invited me to a planning meeting. During the meeting it was decided that a representative should be sent to this year's meeting and since only one other person's schedule would accommodate the trip I was asked to go as well. I accepted and was able to take Patti too. The meeting was to be held in Manila, the Philippines.

Our task was to represent AAPHER as well as the Las Vegas Visitors and Convention Authority, a co-sponsor of the event. As such we were given ten crates of advertising materials and specialty giveaway items and I was given a slot on the agenda on the final day to make the pitch.

We flew to San Francisco in mid July and the temperature dropped from 115 degrees in Las Vegas to 65 in San Francisco, where we boarded a Philippine Airlines 747 and headed across the water. A scheduled stop in Guam was overflown because none of the passengers ended their journey there.

We finally arrived in Manila and were escorted to a hotel next to the Convention Center. There had been an international Travel Agent convention at the Manila Convention Center several months earlier and a bomb had exploded in the Convention Center. That event caused Ferdinand Marcos to place the country under Martial Law.

Security was very tight and each time we entered the hotel we went through security that included a full body pat down. A security guard patrolled each floor of the hotel.

The convention began, and we set up our tables with key chains, pamphlets, plastic bags, and other Las Vegas giveaway paraphernalia, but few people came by our table and nobody who came by took anything. After an hour or so I left Patti to go to the rest room. When I returned I heard a scuffle and ran toward our table. I saw Patti pinned against the wall by a mob pushing the table against her and grabbing the free gifts. I raced toward the crowd and in one leap jumped atop the table and shouted. "EVERYBODY GET BACK! FORM A LINE OR YOU WILL RECEIVE NOTHING!" As quickly as they had rushed the tables, the mob immediately formed an orderly line, and we straightened the tables. Patti was shaking and I asked what happened. She said that one person came to the tables, picked up a few items and asked, "How much?" She said it was free and the person turned to the crowd and yelled something in an Asian language and the rest of the people made a mad rush to the table. Apparently they thought the giveaways were for purchase.

By this time security guards had gathered around the table and the director of the local organization had arrived and was apologizing profusely. She was a high school principal whose name was Chit, and she invited us to her house for dinner that evening to make up for the faux pas, and to see some Philippine culture. We agreed and she said she would be in front of the hotel with her driver at 7:00 p.m. to pick us up.

At 7:00 sharp a Mercedes pulled up and Chit got out to greet us. I noticed that flags were mounted on the front fenders of the car and did not know what to make of that. We drove through the crowded streets and beggars, some who were naked children, tapped on our window as Chit waved them away. We eventually went through a set of gates and up to her house. During the ride Chit explained that Imelda Marcos's youngest sister, who was also a teacher, had set up the conference. Schools had been closed and all teachers were required to attend and, that is why it was so well attended.

As we exited the Mercedes, a staff of servants was lined up to greet us. The house was beautiful and posh. The food was a feast. We were showered with gifts and I embarrassedly gave a handful of trinkets, Las Vegas souvenirs, in return. Chit apologized that her husband was not home yet, as he was working late.

Dinner, complete with local delicacies, was over when Chit's husband arrived and apologized. He asked if we would like a tour of the "Real" Manila, and of course we said yes. His driver again got into the Mercedes with the flags on the fenders and we went to many places few tourists get to see. We visited a now-closed prison where prisoners were held in cells below sea level. When the tide came in, water filled the cells and the prisoners were drowned. We ended up at the Philippine Hotel, a grand Five-Star palace. It was about 11:00 p.m. by then, and the dining room had been closed, but reopened for us at the husband's request. We had after-dinner desserts and drinks and the finest cigars.

Our host then asked if we would like to see the suite occupied by General MacArthur when he directed the Allied forces. He took us to the suite, not open to the public, which was kept exactly as MacArthur had left it. It was an overwhelming experience and we later learned that our host was the head of the Philippine equivalent of the CIA.

The day the convention was to close I was invited to the dais to say a few words. It was time to officially invite the conference to Las Vegas for the following year. One of the things I had been given upon my arrival was a booklet that included English words and their Tagalog (Ta ga' log—the language of the Philippines) equivalent. Since languages come easily to me, I wrote a paragraph or so in English then translated it phonetically into Tagalog. When I spoke, I thanked our wonderful hosts and invited the group to plan their next convention in Las Vegas. Then I finished my speech with two paragraphs in Tagalog, for which I received a standing ovation.

The next day we gathered our bags and I asked our floor security man, with whom we had become acquainted, how many children he had. He told me and I counted out Las Vegas tee shirts for him, his wife, and children and handed them to him. He looked alarmed and said that the hotel manager would think he had stolen them and he would lose his job. So I wrote a note stating that I had given him the tee shirts as a gift, and signed my name. He thought that would get him off the hook.

As we got downstairs to the lobby Chit was waiting with several young girls. She said, "Patti told me you do not have a house maid so I brought you several to choose from. They all have had thorough background checks and are all trained domestics. This is my gift to you."

I was speechless and said; "We can't just bring people into the country. There is a long waiting list for people to enter"

Chit said that was no problem, that they would be flown to Nellis Air Force Base in Las Vegas and we'd simply pick them up. Patti thanked her for her kindness but said that it just would not work. And with that Chit dismissed the girls, escorted us to her Mercedes and accompanied us to the airport. She had upgraded our tickets to First Class, and we were the only passengers in First Class except for a basketball player who was returning to the U.S. from an exhibition in Manila. We shared the First Class cabin with Kareem Abdul Jabbar, his wife and young son. As we entered the cabin, Kareem nodded to us and, in an effort to not seem like the typical Ugly American, I tried to avoid saying something like, "Can I have your autograph?"

Instead, because I had recently seen the movie, "Airplane," in which he played an airline pilot, I said, "I recognized you immediately and let me tell you how relieved I am to know there is another pilot on board in case of emergency." We all had a good laugh, and the ride home culminated one of the most memorable weeks of my life.

Not long after we left the Philippines the Marcos regime was ousted. Chit had a brother who was a doctor in Hawaii and she safely got out. I'm not sure what happened to her husband, but I received a phone call from her saying that she was in Las Vegas and asking if I could help her find work in the local school district. I do not recall whether or not she found work but we have since lost touch with her.

THE NEW SCHOOL KID IN TOWN

The mid-1970s were interesting times for the nation as well as for Las Vegas. The community was growing up. Corporations were replacing the mob in the hotel-casino business, and teachers were leaving town to get advanced degrees because UNLV, as the only game in town, was unwilling or unable to accommodate all of them. Within the school district there existed a power struggle for the bargaining rights of teachers. Both the American Federation of Teachers (AFT) and the National Education Association (NEA) claimed their local organization to be the official representative of the teachers. School District administrators would settle a contract with one of the organizations and the other would refuse to accept the settlement. Both claimed to have the larger membership but neither would show their rolls. A lawsuit to settle the issue went to the state governing body, which issued a decree that only one of the groups would represent the teachers. On a given date, both organizations would be required to show their membership rolls, and whichever had the larger number would be the exclusive representative of the teachers. Since many teachers held dual memberships, that is, membership in both organizations, it promised to be a daunting task to figure out who had the most.

For the next year or so, until the designated date, both groups attempted to recruit (read "seduce") as many teachers for membership as possible. They offered teacher's perks. The NEA cut deals with hotels to provide teachers with comp meals and shows. The AFT took a different tack, bringing in a university from Florida to offer teachers advanced degrees at an institution other than UNLV.

Nova University was the brainchild of Harvard educator and professor Dr. Abe Fischler. Dr. Fischler believed that educators who completed advanced degrees should be able to do so with practical rather than theoretical degrees. He reasoned that a large segment of those who would pursue Doctorates in the field of Education were working administrators who had little need for theory, but would find a program that addressed practical current-day issues with working solutions, to be valuable. It was a cutting edge concept.

A well to do family had donated a large amount of land to the state of Florida during World War II. The site had been used for various war-related activities but after the war ended the land sat empty. The charter for the land stated that it could only be used for specific endeavors, one of which was education.

Fischler assembled a cadre of financial backers in the mid-1960s, and began a university on the donated land. However, his university would be as non-traditional as had been his idea of a practical Doctorate for working administrators. Instead of building a university from the bottom up; first a bachelor's program, then a master's then a doctorate, Fischler would start a school that taught only Doctoral students who were educational administrators and practitioners. Later he added Masters degrees and then undergraduate programs. Later still a high school was added, then elementary and pre-schools and finally adult education classes. Word was that the educational programs at Nova University could provide educational programs from "the womb to the tomb."

Fishler's concept sent shock waves throughout traditional education. Further, once Nova University was up and running and accredited, the school became even more cutting edge by replicating the program in other geographical areas. That is, he modeled his university after state college formats in the sense that he would take his university to various communities and offer courses taught in rented space, such as high schools and office buildings. However, he did this not only throughout the state of Florida, but also throughout the country. Many upstart universities including Kaplan, National University and the University of Phoenix would copy Fischler's format.

Of course since it was the first to use such an innovative

format, Nova University met with strong resistance everywhere it went, as the university challenged the sovereignty of the local institutions. States tried to ban the school and the concept but Fischler and Nova persevered and soon had satellite sites in multiple states. They had formed a cooperative agreement with the powerful Dade County AFT and by the mid-1970s had added a Masters program for teachers.

That is how it happened that the AFT and their powerful arm in Dade County brought Nova University to Las Vegas in 1978. The announcement of their arrival was made in July. A new university was coming to town. A local union official, Ben Knowles, was hired to be the site administrator and three key administrators from the main Nova University site in Florida came to Las Vegas to interview faculty.

Officials at the two state institutions of higher education in Nevada were caught off guard when Nova was officially licensed in the state. Once the school was up and running, however, an ongoing vicious smear campaign was waged against Nova. Rumors ran rampant that Nova was not accredited (it was), and that Nova's credits would not be accepted by the school district for teacher advancement (they were). Nova withstood the barrage and slowly became a force on the education scene in Southern Nevada by providing an option for students that was otherwise not available.

My Doctorate had been completed at UNLV, and I was set to receive my degree in the August 1978 commencement. I had read about Nova coming to town and applied for a part time faculty position. Offices were in the AFT union office complex on Industrial Road, about two blocks from the Whittlesea Taxi and Limousine Company. Classrooms were rented at Las Vegas High School. The non-traditional teaching format called for classes to be held Friday, all day Saturday and Sunday for four consecutive weekends in order to be convenient for teachers. The total number of clock hours over a four-week period met the accreditation time requirement for a three-credit graduate class, and did not interfere with high school classes at Las Vegas High School.

The three administrators from Florida were happy to see me. Their policy was to only hire faculty with Doctoral degrees and I was the first one with that credential who showed up for an interview. I was hired on the spot – the first faculty member to be hired by Nova University at the Las Vegas site. The interviewers were able to cobble together a few other faculty members to form a staff and we opened for business the fall semester, 1978. The response by local teachers was overwhelming. We filled all our classes and had waiting lists for more.

Prior to 1978, many educators in Las Vegas had not pursued master's degrees for reasons such as scheduling, issues with UNLV, or other reasons. Many coaches and single parents were unable to meet the traditional course schedule at UNLV, which offered only evening classes Monday through Thursday to accommodate working educators. With no other post-graduate options available in Las Vegas, a large backlog of teachers that wished to have a graduate degree but were unable to do so, had accumulated. The result was that once word got out that an alternative option to UNLV was available, Nova University was inundated with applicants for the spring semester.

In the early years of Nova's entry into the Southern Nevada higher education scene, many at UNLV viewed Nova as the enemy. One particular Dean of Education at UNLV even lobbied the state legislature to shut Nova down in Nevada. But the need that existed for an alternative to serve the local teachers was so strong that the pushback by the more established university eventually quieted to a simmer.

In the 1970s few people used credit cards. Checks were usually the preferred method of payment transaction in most parts of the country. In Las Vegas, however, due to the transient nature of residents, individual merchants accepted checks reluctantly. That is, in order pay by check, credit must have been established, even at local grocery stores. Thus, the preferred method of paying in Las Vegas was cash, for everything from groceries to tuition.

Site Administrator Ben Knowles had been born and reared in Henderson, a Las Vegas suburb. He was probably in his mid 30s, balding, and wore thick glasses. Unbeknownst to most, Ben had, at that stage in his life, become addicted to gambling. Word was that he had borrowed money from loan sharks who were threatening his well-being. One semester, after a weekend of collecting tuition, instead of locking the money in the safe for later deposit, Ben gathered it all up and disappeared. He has been neither seen nor heard from since.

The three administrators in Florida who had set up the

Las Vegas site and hired me were shocked and dumfounded. Nova had taken several hits in the media and been sanctioned in Michigan, Illinois, and other states that had tried to keep them out. UNLV was nipping at their heels in an effort to drive them out of town, and the last thing they needed was more bad publicity in Las Vegas or anywhere else. They were determined to keep the theft of tuition out of the papers and continue to operate as close to normally as possible.

I received a phone message at my school to go immediately to the Nova offices. As soon as I was able I did so, and made a conference call to the three administrators in Florida. They briefed me and said, "You are the most senior staff member in Las Vegas so you will have to take the position of site administrator."

I graciously declined, explaining that I just had too much on my plate at the time. I was teaching school during the day, working as a quasi-administrator, and teaching Nova classes on the weekends. I simply did not have the time to be a site administrator. When they realized I would not move from that position, they asked if there was anybody I could recommend for the position. I immediately thought of and mentioned Steve Rudish. They said, "Fine, tell him that he's hired."

My response was that they should wait to see if he is willing to take the position but they said they were relieved that we had a solution and that I was to speak to nobody about the missing tuition. I called Steve and he reluctantly agreed to become the site administrator for a little while. The "little while" turned into a 30-year stint.

Full disclosure: Steve Rudish is my cousin. He is five years my junior. When I left home to attend college, the first boy in the clan to do so, Steve was an eighth grader who delivered newspapers after school. He would send me his tip money enclosed in letters, telling me he knew college cost lots of money and he hoped this would help.

Steve grew into a strapping, fine looking young man and a terrific athlete. He was a star football, baseball, and basketball player in high school but his grades were as poor as mine had been at his age. Several college coaches had looked at him but few offered much due to his poor grades.

By the time Steve had graduated from high school, I was living in Pocatello, Idaho. My father had learned from the Mormon missionaries who rented an apartment from him, that there was a Mormon Junior College in Rexburg, Idaho. He asked me to take the scrapbook that Steve's mother had kept, that included Steve's football exploits, to the college athletic department to see if they might be interested in recruiting him. I did and they were. Steve went to Ricks College in Rexburg, Idaho and played baseball and basketball on scholarship. He then transferred to BYU to finish his degree, but injuries to his ankle prevented him from participating in athletics at BYU. His academic pursuits in college, much like my own, were much more successful than they had been in high school.

By the time Steve had graduated from BYU in 1969, I was living in Las Vegas and the local school district was hiring. Steve applied and was immediately hired as an elementary school physical education teacher. However, after a couple of years he decided to leave teaching for the business world. After a few years in the business world, including working as a plant manager at a Levi Strauss Distribution Center in Henderson, he decided to return to the field of education and completed his Masters program. The transition to Nova site administrator took place as he continued to teach in the Clark County School District. He later became a principal but still maintained his position as Nova's Site Administrator. Steve's outside experience in business and his educational background proved to be valuable assets as he guided Nova University, Las Vegas through several cycles of feast and famine.

A NEW FAMILY MEMBER

At some point in the 1980s I received a call from my sister Kathy. She told me of a telephone call that she had received out of the blue. To the best of her recollection it was from Florida, but she was so shaken she could not remember all the details. In short, a woman had phoned her and said that she was a long lost half-sister. The woman said she had been born in Pittsburgh and at age 18 months was adopted by a childless couple and reared as an only child. One day, when she was a teen and her parents were away for the evening, she set out to explore possible hiding places for holiday gifts. What she found instead were her adoption papers. Up to that time she had not realized she had been adopted. When her parents arrived home they confirmed that she had indeed been adopted from a convent in Pittsburgh. We later discovered her name was Evelyn.

Eventually the excitement and imagination of "Who am

I?" was placed on a back burner and Evelyn got on with her life. She married and had a passel of children. Her husband's work took the family from Pittsburgh to Chicago then to Florida, where she and her husband reared their children to adulthood.

Once most of her children were gone and she had some free time, Evelyn began to research her own birth and adoption records and discovered that her biological father was the same as my own biological father. Her biological mother, ironically, lived in Florida, not far from her own home. She phoned both biological parents but neither wanted to discuss or pursue the issue. Evelyn's birth had taken place in 1938, a time when childbirth to a single mother was just not discussed. Evelyn told Kathy, during their initial telephone conversation, that she was preparing for the Christmas holidays with her own family and wanted to know if they could talk again after the holidays.

Kathy phoned me to relate her experience and to get my thoughts on the matter. I was of course suspicious, a natural reaction to such a story. Still, we brainstormed and wondered "What if?" After all, young people are only human. I suppose it WAS possible. I asked Kathy if she remembered the woman's name, phone number, or where she lived in Florida and Kathy said she was so stunned by the conversation that she took no notes. We both wondered if the mysterious person would call back, if it were a hoax, or if it was somebody who simply was a crank.

Christmas came and went with no phone call and we

began to think it had been a hoax, when Kathy received another call from the same person. She confirmed that her name was Evelyn, and she had all the proper documentation to support her story. She further said that she was active in an organization of adoptees that sought out their birth parents and siblings in an effort to establish relationships and family health history, as well as genealogical information.

Our other two siblings were not interested in pursuing the matter so Kathy and I and our spouses flew to Florida to meet Evelyn and her family. We still wondered if it might be a hoax and therefore moved forward with caution.

The moment we met Evelyn, however, there was no further doubt. Not only did she have the official documentation to support her story, she was the spitting image of our aunt, my father's sister. Her husband was a warm fellow and her kids, and there was a passel, including twin boys, were all bright and successful. One daughter is an engineer, another a nurse, a son is a TV personality; another son is developing a school in Indonesia, and on and on. They are a wonderful family and Evelyn is an amazing person.

THE ACCIDENTAL
COLUMNIST

It did not take long after the completion of my Doctoral degree to become antsy, despite teaching weekend classes at Nova. My next challenge came in another unexpected manner. As I read a man-about-town column the local newspaper one morning said to Patti, "I can write better than this hack."

She said, "Why don't you?"

I had been only half serious but soon my wheels began to turn. After all, I had been the accidental college student, accidental teacher, accidental taxi and limo driver, accidental school administrator, accidental college professor.... why not the accidental newspaper columnist? We brainstormed for a while and I said, "Aside from one journalism class my freshman year and the published article in college that got my father into trouble, I've never written for a paper."

Patti's response was, "You know Brian. Call him and ask what he thinks."

An excellent suggestion!

Brian Greenspun, son of Hank, the editor and owner of the Las Vegas Sun Newspaper, was an editor at the paper. Brian and Patti had been high school classmates and we'd seen him socially from time to time over the years. So I put a call into him.

When he answered I told him my thoughts about the man-about-town column. He said, "This is fate! We just completed a staff meeting on that very the topic. We are looking for somebody local who could write a light, humorous, column that people would enjoy over their morning coffee. Write up a half-dozen columns—500 words each—and send them to me. I am not interested in the accuracy or the content at this point. I just want to see your style."

I did as Brian asked and wrote up seven 500-word columns and dropped them off at his office. Then heard nothing for several weeks and I thought, "Oh well."

However, the call eventually came with Brian's apologies. Several of the people whose approval was needed had been on staggered vacation schedules and it had taken until now to get all the feedback – which was unanimous. "We want you to write and we'll pay you $75 per column, which is the most any columnist is earning at the newspaper." I was smitten.

"Ok, I'll do it. Today is Friday, When do I start?"

"Monday. Your copy must be turned in by Sunday at 5:00 p.m. so it can be put up."

"This Monday?"

"Yes."

"Ok, how often do you want the column to appear?" (Thinking monthly perhaps).

"Three days per week—Monday, Wednesday, and Friday. You need to come down today to have your picture taken for the masthead. You will be on page one of the Local section."

My ego was going wild. "What about a name for my column? I would like to call it 'Vegascellaneous,' as in Miscellaneous Las Vegas."

Brian laughed as though I were joking. "Right! First, that word is too long to fit on the masthead and second, our readership reads on the eighth grade level, and would have no clue what that means. Don't worry. We'll come up with a name."

And so it was that the following Monday morning, "Nixon's Nook" was born.

That night the UNLV Rebel basketball team had a home game. At the time they played their home games at the Las Vegas Convention Center, as there was no place available on campus to accommodate the 6,000-plus fans that were flocking to the arena to follow the new coach, Jerry Tarkanian. Patti and I had season tickets and sat next to a gentlemen and his wife. I was not sure what he did at the time but thought he was in the gaming business at one of the major hotels. I told him of my new job and wondered aloud what I might write for my initial column. He did not say much. At halftime we took our customary walk around the arena. He said he could give me plenty of information for my column but I could never reveal my source. A chill ran up my spine as I began to feel like an investigative reporter and my friend told me the first of many, many stories and tidbits for my column.

He was indeed the comptroller for one of the major hotels. One of their whales (high rollers) was coming to town. This man would arrive in his private jet, a converted Boeing 727, and disembark with his entourage and suitcases packed with cash. It was not uncommon for him to lose millions at the tables. When his money ran out he would return home until his next foray to Las Vegas. The story itself was a good one but it was heightened by two tidbits – first that this million-dollar gambler was hooked on McDonald hamburgers and upon exiting the plane, the Hotel's limo driver was instructed to make his first stop at the nearest McDonald drive-up window where the gambler and his guests loaded up on McDonald's hamburgers for their stay. The second tidbit was that he was the son of the president of an impoverished Latin American country. While the population of the country starved, the corrupt president took their money, and his son gambled and frittered it away in Las Vegas. I wrote my first column around that story and it became a hit from day one.

Another story he gave me was of a newly hired security guard at a downtown hotel. As an initiation rite, the more senior security guards wove scary tales of dimly lit corridors in the hotel. They then sent the newby up to investigate on the premise that they'd gotten a trouble call on one such floor, where they first had surreptitiously dimmed the lights. The jittery security guard got off the elevator at one end of the dark corridor and immediately saw somebody lurking at the other end of the hallway. He placed his hand on his gun and saw that the person on the other end did the same. He drew his gun and the person on the other end did the same. The security guard fired one shot the length of the hallway and it shattered the mirror at the other end. He had shot his own image in the mirror at the end of the hall.

The friend, whose identity I've never revealed, gave me many more tips over the years and introduced me to other sources. I loved writing the column but it was just an avocation. I was a school administrator at the time and a professor on weekends and that was what paid the bills.

I received a press release that UNLV was going to break ground for a new sports arena, and went to the press party that announced the plans. During my mingling, I met the recently hired UNLV Athletic Director, Dr. Brad Rothermel. In my next column I spoke about the new arena and mentioned how lucky we were to have such a competent, energetic athletic director at the helm. The whole bit was only a couple of paragraphs.

Dr. Rothermel phoned me the next day and thanked me for the kind words. I usually only heard from people who were upset with something I'd written. We chatted and I explained that I'm not a journalist but an educator who just happens to write a column. I told him I was a Rebel fan and

UNLV grad and would be happy to help him if I ever could. He said that a new position had just been authorized for an Academic Advisor for Athletics. A football coach had been hired and his contract called for a person to direct academic support services for football. If I was interested, perhaps I should apply.

The position search was a national one so I did not think I'd stand much of a chance but I applied anyhow. The new football coach, Harvey Hyde, interviewed me. He had been a very successful head coach at Pasadena City College and this was his first Division I head coaching assignment. He was late for the interview and talked the entire time. I could barely get a word in edgewise. He said he had no idea what the position would look like but he wanted somebody with a solid academic background to develop it. In addition his only three criteria were to find somebody who had lived in the community a long time (score one for me – a leg up over the out-of-state candidates), somebody with a Doctorate so they could talk the same language as the professors (score two for me), and somebody who had never coached. When he took a breath, I quickly said I met all three criteria, and in fact, not only had I never coached, the most athletic thing I did during college was to shift into second gear – and I usually ground the gears doing it. He missed my attempt at humor but told me there were several local candidates and he would keep me posted.

THE ACCIDENTAL ACADEMIC COACH

The more I thought about the position the more excited I became. Here was a chance to become a university administrator and work in the Athletic Department but be the Academic person, and develop a program. I decided I would go all out after the job and either contacted Coach Hyde or visited him daily. I saw him in his office, on the athletic field, ran into him at his speaking engagements, and so on. Finally he made the decision to hire me, probably so I would quit stalking him, and I took a leave of absence from the school district, since I was not sure whether or not the new position would work out. It was a "soft money" position, which meant it was not funded by the state and, as an "at will" position, was vulnerable to be terminated at any time. Of course, there were some soft money positions that had been in place for decades.

My first day on the job Coach Hyde handed me the 600-page NCAA Handbook and said, "I want you to know this book inside and out. Part of your job will be to keep us out of trouble." It was the summer of 1982 and NCAA Proposition 48 was about to go into effect. It was the most profound rule change regarding academics in athletics up to that time and strengthened academic requirements for college athletes. I spent the summer memorizing the NCAA rulebook and calling the NCAA for interpretations. In the process my name became familiar with some of the compliance members, which was important, as once fall semester began they were so overwhelmed with calls that they often only had time to respond to specific people. Each university could have four designees with permission to make official calls – the Athletic Director, the Faculty Athletic Representative, the university President, and an at large designee. I was the latter.

As the summer wore on Coach Hyde gave me another assignment. He said, "I need you to clear incoming players admissions and review grades for returning players, and be sure that by the first day of practice I have 105 players eligible. If you do that, you can take the next six weeks off. If you want to travel with the team for away games, just show up to the plane. Otherwise you'll have no obligations from me until it is time to track the players' academic performance."

University of Oklahoma graduate Jackie Newton had been the Athletic Academic Advisor for all sports prior to my being hired. She was a great help to me regarding the ebb and flow of academic support services. From her I also learned there was a loosely knit national group of Athletic Academic Advisors and they were scheduled to meet in San Diego in a few weeks. I requested permission to attend the conference but was told there was no budget for travel for my position. So I asked if I could have the time off and I would pay my own way. Permission granted.

It was at that meeting I met the president of the young organization, Dr. Lynn Lashbrook, University of Missouri (later to become the Athletic Director at University of Alaska, and then go into private business). Dr. Gerry Gurney, Iowa State University, would move on to direct programs at Southern Methodist University, University of Maryland, and University of Oklahoma, and Bob Bradley, University of Kentucky. We formed a closely-knit group, and over the next ten-year period, helped shape the face of Athletic Academic Support Services for the NCAA. Each of us became officers in the organization. We wrote legislation, established standards, created a refereed journal (one that had an editorial staff review submissions for publication), and lobbied for the athletes. It was an exciting time of phenomenal growth in NCAA athletics and academics. The small organization of Academic Advisors for Athletics grew from a handful of schools to participation by every major school. Some had just one representative; others had entire staffs devoted to athletic academic support services.

Like my colleagues, I became very active in the field, attending conferences, giving lectures, hosting seminars, serving as journal editor, and writing about the field of academic support services for athletes. On a trip to Northeastern University in Boston to make a presentation I met Dr. Richard Lapchick, son of legendary St. John's basketball coach, Joe Lapchick. Richard was an activist and we immediately became friends. He had been active in the anti-apartheid movement in South Africa. As the result he was attacked outside a public library and a racial epithet carved into his chest. His focus at the time was to help keep the "student" in "Student Athlete." Northeastern had given him office space in the university and, with Richard doing most of the logistical heavy lifting; we developed an institute for the betterment of college athletes. Among other successes we developed an aftercare program for athletes who had completed their eligibility but not their degrees. Each participating university either waived tuition or substantially reduced it in exchange for the returnee doing some sort of community service for the school. Usually that service involved going into the community and speaking to schoolchildren about the importance of a college education. The program helped countless athletes complete their degrees. Richard eventually moved the operation to Central Florida.

Meanwhile, at UNLV, Coach Hyde was showing his success as an excellent coach. He took the team to their school's first ever Division I post season Bowl Game and his team won handily. His players included future NFL stars Randall Cunningham, Ickey Woods, Charles Dimry, and George Thomas to name a few. It seemed the good times would never end. But they did.

The newly appointed college president did not share the vision of the coaches and athletic administrators. He had a very difficult time as the president of a university whose most recognizable employee was the basketball coach. A war developed between his office and the athletic department and the president went on a crusade to bring down the storied basketball program. But basketball was too deeply entrenched at UNLV, so the focus moved to the football program. I will not expound upon all the underhanded things that were done during that reign of terror as they have been chronicled elsewhere. Instead I will simply say the result caused my career in Athletic Administration as well as the coaching careers of some very fine coaches and athletic administrators to come to a premature end. Even now, some three decades later, the programs have not recovered. I left the university 18 months short of having enough time in the state system to retire.

After my position at UNLV was eliminated, I applied for a position at the local community College but was not selected. My only other option was to return to the school district for 18 months in order to qualify for a pension. I applied and was immediately hired as a librarian. I was encouraged by the school district administration to go back into K-12 school administration, but that would have required a year-long District Administrative Selection Program. I chose not to do that and, in addition to my school librarian job, also worked the advertising specialty business. I also continued teaching courses part time for Nova Southeastern and other universities.

THE ACCIDENTAL
BUSINESS OWNER

Coach Hyde and I quickly became friends on a professional level but it would also become a longtime personal friendship that continues until this day. He had kept his house in Pasadena, California while he coached in Las Vegas, and after being fired at UNLV, would return to relax and maintain his Los Angeles area contacts. He has since become a sports radio talk show host.

While coaching football at UNLV, Coach Hyde also spent time in his hometown of Pasadena. On one visit he spoke to an old friend of his, businessman, Peter Bedourian. Peter owned a very successful advertising specialty business in Orange County called Promotional Media. He was looking into the possibility of expanding his business into Las Vegas and asked Harvey if he knew anybody who might be interested in a part time sales position. Harvey thought of me and told me of his conversation with Pete. I knew absolutely nothing about that business but had lived in Las Vegas a long time and knew lots of people. I took a trip to Orange County to talk to Pete.

Pete outlined his vision. He wanted to get into the local hotels, particularly the Strip resorts. They would add status to his client list and make money at the same time. As an outside salesman all I had to do was take the orders, phone them into his office, and his staff would do the rest.

I agreed to give it a try but soon discovered that the local hotels were not the right target audience. First, they were so large that they expected (and got) such concessions from vendors that it was difficult to make money. Secondly, they often were very, very slow to pay and, if a small businessman threatened to sue, they'd laugh and tell him to get to the end of the line behind all the others who had threatened to sue. But Pete insisted I work the hotels so I did and made a few sales.

Somebody had told Patti that the Cowboy Christmas Show that accompanied the National Finals Rodeo (NFR) in December was quite the place to sell products. Patti arranged an interview with Herb McDonald, president of Las Vegas Events, who coordinated the show, and he agreed to give us free space to sell Christmas ornaments with the NFR logo. I called Pete to tell him but he was not interested in taking on that job, so I asked if he minded it I did it on my own. I'd buy the ornaments from him at retail then resell them at the Cowboy Christmas Show at a premium. He agreed, and

I went back to Herb and asked how many bulbs he thought would sell. He said 10,000. I thought that number was a little high and instead ordered 3,000. That episode demonstrated my naïveté regarding the advertising specialty business.

The show was a disaster for us. We sold MAYBE 300 bulbs. I told Pete of the fiasco and expected him to say, "Why don't you just pay me my cost – no profit, and we'll chalk it up to experience." After all, I had been making money for him and established contacts in the casino industry. But he did not say that and we not only took a hit on the huge numbers of ornaments that I'd purchased and did not sell, but we paid Pete his profit to boot. His unwillingness to help me in the matter stuck in my craw, so I said to Patti, "We can do this. Let's start our own company." And we did.

My first sale was to Steve Stallworth, a former quarterback on the UNLV football team who had graduated and gone to work for a local advertising agency. He needed some clear plastic rulers with gold logos, for a local homebuilder. Since I did not have Pete to research manufacturers, I went to the library to find them myself, found one and placed the order. It was a very cumbersome way of doing business but it was a learning experience and it worked. Steve placed several other orders with me, and then his colleagues at the agency began to do so as well. The process to find manufacturers was arduous but I soldiered on. Eventually we did enough business to join the Advertising Specialty Institute, the major industry organization that provides manufacturers, credit histories, and other shortcuts for small businesses. This made the business run much more smoothly.

I soon discovered that my niche for the advertising specialty business was certainly not the hotels, but advertising agencies. Their employees were usually young, very creative, but not too disciplined when it came to deadlines. Therefore, they were often in a panic when ordering. If they needed the product in two weeks, it might normally require a four-week production time. Cost was rarely an issue. So I learned to haggle with manufacturers, offer to pay a premium to skip my orders ahead of others, or bribe them with a weekend in Las Vegas. Thus, when the young, creative geniuses from the agency needed something in a hurry, they began to call me directly instead of requesting bids. My prices were higher than my competitors, but I was able to meet their tight deadlines. I worked the business out of my home, which kept the overhead down. I would teach during the day and begin my business calls after 3:00 p.m. when school let out.

Competition among vendors for hotel business was keen, but with ad agencies, not so much. Advertising agency account managers are constantly in a crisis mode.

Once the goods are delivered, they are billed net 30 (meaning the bill becomes due within 30 days), but they rarely pay their bills before 90 days. The reason is they do not pay until their client pays them. That can creates a cash flow problem for many small businesses, but not for us. First, we had no employees and no overhead, and second, once I determined whom the client of the ad agency was (a fact that often determined how long the agency would take to pay), I simply added the cost of the money into the bid. We were self financed and could wait.

Our largest advertising agency client had a multi-million dollar contract with the Las Vegas Convention and Visitors Authority (LVCVA), and they often ordered products by the tens of thousands. In those instances we would have the product delivered directly to their client, as we had neither the means to transport it nor the space to store it. Soon our part time business profits far outstripped our education salaries.

ACCIDENTAL
MISS UNIVERSE-1991

The people at Las Vegas Events who had suggested the Christmas ornaments to be sold at the Cowboy Christmas Show felt bad about our fiasco. We became friends and they promised to make it up to us. For the next year or so we did a small business with them. One day in 1991 our friend from Las Vegas Events called and told us the following story: The Miss Universe contest was a huge operation run by a company affiliated with Madison Square Garden in New York. Each year the pageant rotated to a different country. A New York advertising agency usually handled all the logo-related items connected with the pageant. That year, however, an Asian country that was to host the pageant encountered political unrest, so they cancelled and had forfeited their $2 million good faith money deposit. Las Vegas Events had secured the pageant—a first for Las Vegas—but from the day of the signing of the contract to the date of the pageant was only 90 days – as opposed to the year or more lead-time for planning.

The corporation that owned the pageant asked Las Vegas Events to identify a vendor to sell Miss Universe paraphernalia. Our contact at Las Vegas Events asked if we were interested and I said of course. She said there was meeting that afternoon with Miss Universe Corporate and invited us to attend. I phoned Patti at school and told her to hurry home as we had a meeting to attend regarding the business. We headed for the meeting and I was very evasive about it's purpose. After the pageant officials made a very fine and professional presentation, the pageant representative asked if we would be willing to bid on the job. I said, "I'm not sure what to bid. We have not done a beauty contest or pageant before"

The representative said, "It doesn't matter. You will get the bid. Just be fair with us. Due to the limited lead time, I expressed to the Las Vegas Events people that we need somebody who can deliver, who is trustworthy, and who will still be here after the pageant to pay the bills. They said your company was the first one on their list, so we are asking you to vend for us."

He then outlined the products that are usually sold; posters, jewelry, tee shirts, sweatshirts, silk jackets, and other apparel. The jewelry and posters had already been assigned to vendors with long-term contracts but the rest, including anything we would like to include, would be at our discretion. There is a royalty on every item with a logo, and they expected us to monitor sales and submit the royalty fees within 60 days after the event. We agreed, Patti and I signed the papers, and we left.

After the meeting, as Patti walked to the car in a trance, she said, "What the Hell did we just do? I have no idea what to order, how many, how we'll pay for it...."

I reassured her it would be fine. I had done some research prior to the meeting and learned that the forerunner to the pageant was Miss USA, which had just been held in Kansas City. I would phone them, see what they had ordered, add 10 percent to the order, and we'd survive.

Dominic Clark was a longtime Las Vegan who had at one time been the UNLV Director of Sports Information. He and Patti attended college together and he owned a company that had been given the contract to do the programs. Dominic phoned me and said that the advertising for the programs had paid for all their costs, but they needed to be sold. He would provide them to us at no cost and we would split the revenue they generated 60/40. No investment. That was good. We agreed. When the date for the pageant rolled around we were ready. The programs were one of our biggest sellers. Everybody bought one for themselves and others to take home as souvenirs.

The Miss Universe Pageant was held at the Aladdin Hotel (now Planet Hollywood) Theater. We were given an entire room – the former poker room that was about to be remodeled, to display and sell our wares. Patti and her best friend Teresa Moy set up a display that would have made Nordstrom proud. Contestants and their entourages began to arrive Saturday, a week before the pageant. Sales were slow but steady. We gave the contestants a discount for good will and to stimulate sales.

I had taken the entire week off from UNLV, using vacation time, and set up every morning at 9:00 a.m. Patti would come in after school. By the following Thursday we had only sold a small percentage of our inventory and I was beginning to worry but did not want to worry Patti. To make matters worse, the poster and jewelry vendor walked past Patti's beautiful display, did a double take and said, "What the Hell do you think you're doing? They will steal you blind!" He then calmed down and explained that only one of each item should be on display. The rest needed to be behind the table where the mobs, and he assured us there would be mobs, did not have access.

Thursday was a free dress rehearsal and the public was invited. Sales picked up dramatically. However it was nothing compared to what lay ahead the night of the pageant, which was broadcast worldwide in prime time.

The chaos inside the hotel on pageant night was indescribable. Sales started in the early afternoon as people began arriving. The sales continued to escalate and overwhelm our little display that had seemed so big before that night. We were taking money for merchandise and just throwing it into empty t-shirt cartons. I had taken a room in the hotel that night in case we worked late, and also asked for a lock box at the cashier's window to keep the cash. When the t-shirt box would begin to fill with cash, I loaded my pockets and every other orifice that was available, and walked to the lock box to make a deposit. I was so loaded with cash that I had to walk like a penguin so as not to drop any money. I made multiple trips, stuffing tens, twenties, fifties, and hundreds, into the lock box. When the smoke had cleared and the pageant was over, we had sold every single item except for a couple of hundred sweatshirts. It was May and the weather was warm in Las Vegas, and under those conditions sweatshirts were just not big sellers. Lupita Jones (pronounced Hon'es) from Mexico was crowned Miss Universe but the small local advertising specialty company of Promotions By Pat was also victorious.

We made more money that week, even after all expenses and royalties were paid, than Patti and I did together for a year in education. The ad specialty business was good. The special event business was awesome! When the pageant returned to Las Vegas in 1995 we made a formal bid and just squeaked past a San Francisco firm for the contract. That was another successful endeavor.

ARMS AND LEGS EVERY-WHERE – NO ACCIDENT

One day I received a call from Jill Blanchette, one of the account executives at the ad agency with whom I worked so closely. She was working on a project and needed help. A local hospital was adding a new state-of-the-art surgical wing and children's wing. They planned to have a weeklong open house to show off the facility and introduce it to the public. They wanted mannequins dressed as doctors, nurses, and patients including children to simulate the actual work that was to be done in the surgical wing. She had gone to the local display company that had given her a price of their mannequins to rent for $1,000 per mannequin per week. She estimated they would need about 25 mannequins and rental of mannequins would exceed her budget. She phoned me and asked if I would be able to secure anything for less money. I said, "of course," and proceeded to give myself a crash course in mannequins.

It turned out that there were only two places in the world where mannequins that looked like people were still manufactured—France and Asia. There was not much of a market at the time for human-looking mannequins because most store mannequins were abstract, and Jill's client needed articulating mannequins (those whose arms and legs could be moved into various positions). Also, as the civil rights movement became a part of the fabric of society, a question of skin color became an issue. Since nearly all mannequins up to that time had been sort of a neutral pink color, and since customers were becoming more diverse, the industry solved the problem by side-stepping it and making avant-garde looking statues with silver, half heads, and no bodies. The articulated mannequin markets were simply not available at the time. No wonder the display company charged a premium for them.

My logic was that if all the top-level stores and chic boutiques were using the new wave statues, somebody must still be using the old style, and if so somebody had to repair and refurbish them. I spent two days researching the topic and found a few such places. One was called Jose's, which was located in Ontario, California, a three-hour drive from Las Vegas. I phoned and spoke to Jose and told him what I needed—adults, children, males, females, Hispanic, African-American, Causation, and Asian. Jose said he could accommodate all of the requests. However, he was not willing to ship them. I must come to Ontario and pick them up and deliver them when finished. I explained that I had a Lincoln

Continental and he said the trunk and back seat would easily hold parts for 25 of the fiberglass people. He would give me a lesson on how to reassemble them. We agreed on a price and I was able to save Jill more than half off her original bid and still make a very handsome profit.

Because of the huge savings from the mannequins, Jill now had a budget with a substantial amount of the funding left over, so she phoned again and said she'd like to present a gift to everybody who visited the open house. The gift would have to be gender and age neutral and be easily distributed and non-perishable. Patti and I brainstormed and came up with the following: each visitor would receive a little packet that included a pencil with the logo and phone number of the hospital, a pad of note paper with the logo and phone number, and a pocket calculator with the logo and phone number. Since the theme of the new wing was diamonds, we found a calculator with clear Lucite buttons that looked like diamonds. Jill ordered 10,000 of each item. The deal was a home run for the business.

We set up and dressed the mannequins and the open house went perfectly. As we walked through the hospital with the dissembled parts, people gave us strange looks. I just shrugged and said, "Spare parts for surgery" and continued walking. One week later the arms, legs, and torsos were returned to Jose and everybody was happy.

THE ACCIDENTAL PROFESSOR

While working at UNLV, then the school district, I had also been teaching courses for several universities – UNLV, Lesley University, Nova Southeastern, and others. All were part time gigs. In fact, I had been teaching for Nova off and on since 1978 when they first came to Las Vegas. After my UNLV assignment expired, I took a position with the school district as a librarian. I could see that I was being groomed to reenter the school administrator's domain, however, I saw other opportunities outside the school district that were more to my liking. The advertising specialty business was picking up and I was still able to teach part time at Nova Southeastern (Nova had attempted to buy a medical school in North Miami Beach, Southeastern University. The school administration agreed but insisted on keeping the name so Nova University became Nova Southeastern University). I thought I would probably continue with the business and maybe teach an occasional university class. The administrators at Nova told me that whenever I left the school district and UNLV, there would always be a position for me with them. I kept that option in my hip pocket for the moment.

One of my favorite teaching assignments was with Lesley University (then Lesley College). Lesley is a small school whose most famous aspect is its location, next door to Harvard in Boston. But they had a unique outreach program. Their specialty was master's degree programs for teachers. They would hire a recruiter in an area that was either not served or underserved by local colleges and universities. The recruiter put together cohorts of 25-30 teachers and the college would fly professors to the site. A three-credit course was presented in a manner similar to the delivery of Nova's cutting edge format from years earlier and that of Northern Arizona University in Kingman in 1972. That is, a faculty member would fly in early Friday afternoon; teach Friday evening, all day Saturday, and Sunday morning. The class would be taught one weekend each month for three consecutive months then a paper or project would be due in lieu of the fourth meeting. I taught classes for Lesley in this manner in Helena, Montana, Las Cruses, New Mexico, Spokane, Washington and even Las Vegas. It was fun duty as there was always time to explore after class.

Once I retired from the school district in 1994 Nova began to use me more and more frequently. They had added an undergraduate degree and graduate teacher licensure program to their Las Vegas offerings and put me in charge of the student teaching component. Remember, I had never student taught!

The multiple part time jobs piled up until my class load exceeded that of a full time professor. I finally said, "Enough! Either hire me full time with benefits or replace me." They hired me as a full time student-teacher liaison and I continued teaching part time. Since the main campus is in Fort Lauderdale, Florida, there was a substantial amount of travel between Las Vegas and Fort Lauderdale. On one visit I found my way to the department that housed the Educational Leadership Doctoral Program. I met with Dr. Charlie Faires who had played football at Northern Arizona University decades earlier. He showed me a map and pointed out where all the Nova Southeastern University Doctoral program sites were located around the country and indicated a new one that was penciled in for Chicago.

After looking at his chart I said, "You already have two programs in Chicago, why not bring one to Las Vegas"

He looked blankly and said, "Why? What would be the benefit to us?"

I gave him the 20-minute version of the Las Vegas Chamber of Commerce routine – how Vegas is the fastest growing city in the country and is projected to continue, how Nova's highest grossing site outside Florida is Las Vegas, and how much he would enjoy coming to Las Vegas to monitor the program. When I stopped for a breath he said, "I'm sold. Would you be the Site Administrator for the Education

Leaders Doctoral Program? Because if you recruit students like you just recruited me, we will make a fortune!"

I agreed, and soon my duties at Nova Southeastern University in Las Vegas included: being a full time administrator for the student teaching program, a part time professor in the Educational Administration Master's Degree program, and now, the part time Site Administrator for the Doctorate in Educational Leadership. On the side I was still working the ad specialty business.

I was soon given an assistant to help with the Doctoral program and began to rapidly create cohorts for that program. The format was similar to the one used by Lesley College and other schools as defined above. I recruited and managed each cohort and was paid for each cohort. The program grew beyond even my wildest expectations and soon I had about a dozen cohorts to manage. That not only made me a very highly paid person, but also gave an opportunity for many school administrators to complete a terminal degree, and made Dr. Faires and the budget people in Florida very, very happy.

Meanwhile, back on the main Fort Lauderdale campus, a group of administrators was sitting in a room reviewing the Doctoral programs and the people who served as Site Administrators. One of the "professionals" squealed and said, "Lord! Do you realize how much money Andy Nixon makes as a part time Site Administrator?" And she blurted out my pay amount from the previous year. Another administrator looked at the document and said, "He makes more than I do. He is a part time Site Administrator and I'm a vice president! That can't be allowed to happen." Soon, my finances were the buzz of the Fort Lauderdale Administration. It did not matter that for every cohort I established, and for every dollar they paid me, $100 flowed to the university. It did not matter that the revenue I was generating was paying their salaries. All that mattered to them was that they had a more prestigious title than did I, yet I was earning more money than were they. They scoured the records and discovered a colleague in Alabama who was making nearly as much as I was, for she too was an excellent recruiter. We two were summoned to Florida to get the problem resolved.

The resolution was to limit Site Administrators to a maximum of three cohorts at any given time. The number of cohorts at Las Vegas (worth about $3 million per cohort to the school) dwindled from twelve, to six to three, as students completed their degree programs. The full time administrators in Florida were once again earning more money than the two part time Site Administrators in Las Vegas and Alabama, but the program was plunging into debt. Eventually the department was purged of most of the administrators who had complained but it was too late to recreate what had once been a cash cow for the university and a service to local administrators. By that time I had moved on, and the Internet was becoming the delivery system of choice by many seeking advanced degrees. Nova Southeastern still maintains a presence in Las Vegas with a small contingent of employees, but most local students do most of their studies online.

Nova was and is an asset to Las Vegas and my 30-year association with the school led to much professional growth and self-satisfaction. I am hopeful that I was able to provide the means for a solid education for educators and others who chose to enhance their academic credentials and skills.

THE ACCIDENTAL CONSULTANT

As my career in higher education began to wind down, I began to look toward other areas in which I could apply my skills. Several possibilities arose. Two of my Doctoral students at Nova Southeastern University, DaJaun and Tamara Anderson had come to Las Vegas from Michigan. They both accepted positions at the Andre Agassi College Preparatory Academy (AACPA), a charter school in Las Vegas. The school was built in the center of a depressed socio-economic part of town. Children who lived in the area were often impoverished and the area had a high dropout rate. Andre's vision was to provide a school with the resources and support that would encourage graduates to become successful in life, get a college education, and give something back to the community.

I had visited AACPA several times to observe my Doctoral

students and was invited to consult on a committee that was planning to expand the school to include a high school. From that experience I was invited to be a Board member at the school, which I accepted. The two students completed their programs of study, rose through the administrative ranks, married, and moved on to start their own school in another part of the country. Dr. DaJuan Anderson and Dr. Tamara Anderson made huge contributions to AACPA as teachers and administrators. I continued as a Board member at AACPA for several years as the school grew from its humble beginning with grades three, four, and five, to a full-fledged K-12 charter school. I watched with pride the first graduating class commencement and every member of the class went on to higher education.

David Monroe, another former doctoral student phoned me one day and stated that he was part of a group who wanted to provide further education by starting a college. He and the members of his planning committee were well versed in their fields but needed help in structuring the school. He asked me if I would help by serving as a consultant and of course I said that I would be happy to. The school was started from scratch, and filled a very important need in the field. Unfortunately there were some glitches in the basic structure, and the school did not thrive and prosper as we had hoped.

While working at UNLV I struck up a friendship with one of the professors in the College of Business. Ed Joyce and I have maintained that friendship for nearly 30 years and have been involved with many business and consulting ventures during that time. One such venture was launched when he phoned me and asked if I would speak to a group of investors who wanted to develop a medical school in Latin American country. Since I was fresh off developing another school I agreed. I made the presentation to the group that consisted of doctors and businessmen who were native to Guatemala, but who were American citizens, and wanted to give back to their homeland. They liked the presentation and soon I was off to a visit to Universidad Galileo in Guatemala City. The group wanted to expand the offerings of the university and my position was to help put a plan together that would facilitate the addition of graduate courses.

I turned to Dr. David Monroe, my former Doctoral student who had developed the aforementioned college, and we put together a plan that was successfully implemented at Universidad Galileo. My visits to Guatemala helped me nurture a love for a country. I had never previously visited Guatemala but discovered that her beauty exceeds that of many other countries. Her people are kind, generous, and hard workers.

My trips to Guatemala provided other benefits and opportunities to expand my life experiences. As a consulting team we were treated almost like royalty. We were given the executive conference room in the administration building at Galileo to do our work. All needed resources were provided and the environment at Universidad Galileo was one of the most lush and beautiful that I had ever seen. The campus abutted another university, Universidad Marroquin, a private university that is considered the most elite of the country. It also had gardens, large expanses of greenery, and together the two campuses formed an ambience reminiscent of Shangri-La.

The president of the Universidad Galileo, Dr. Eduardo Suger came to the conference room the end of our first day there. He said to me that he was going to make a brief presentation over the school TV network, and then we would talk. His presentation was to be broadcast throughout Guatemala.

The cameras came on and the president began to speak. He was so eloquent that I leaned to the Provost who was sitting next to me, and said, "That sounds like a campaign speech."

He said, "It is."

I asked, "What is he campaigning for?"

"The presidency."

"Of what?"

"Guatemala."

Here I was in the same room as a presidential candidate. Dr. Suger did not win the presidency but ran a respectable second or third in a field of 16 candidates.

Dr. Estuardo Zachrisson, a renowned dentist, also hosted us. Dr. Zachrisson came from a prominent Guatemalan family (his grandfather's picture is on Guatemala's currency) and is an international speaker in the area of pediatric dentistry. He has a home and practice in Guatemala City as well as a home in Antigua, the original capital of Guatemala.

Dr. Zachrisson gave us tours of a Guatemala that we would never have otherwise seen. Those mentioned here are just of the few of the wonderful people I met in Guatemala.

When I was initially invited to speak to the group of Guatemalan Americans, one of the businessmen who would underwrite part of the proposal was Jose Fernando Garcia. Fernando and Ed Joyce had something in common as both their sons graduated from the U.S. Naval Academy in Annapolis. Fernando became a very close friend and we continue to meet regularly for lunch.

THE ACCIDENTAL
NAVAL OFFICER

I had come close to serving in the military on several occasions but somehow always missed by a whisker. As a freshman in college I joined the BYU USAF ROTC but was told by a student officer that I lacked the discipline to be an officer. I had taken a test on which I scored well enough to be a navigator but not a pilot, so I dropped out of the Air Force ROTC program. During my senior year in college I was offered a commission in the Army Medical Corps as a psychologist but did not follow through. After I graduated and began teaching I nearly went into Naval Aviation training, but backed out at the last minute. Early in my first marriage I applied for pilot training in the Army but failed the physical. The Army physician told me I had a hearing deficiency that would preclude me from flying in the military. So it was that I would not serve my country's military service – or so I thought.

My good friend and fellow UNLV professor Ed Joyce phoned me one day and asked if I would consider an appointment as a Blue and Gold Officer for the U.S. Naval Academy (USNA) in Annapolis. I asked him exactly what that meant and he explained that a Blue and Gold Officer is an extension of the Naval Academy Admissions Office. When a high school student indicates an interest in the USNA, that person is assigned to a local Blue and Gold Officer (BGO) who helps the applicant package his/herself for formal application, guides them through the process, interviews and evaluates them, and otherwise provides assistance and direction. The process requires a weeklong training session on the U.S. Naval Academy campus at Annapolis. I completed the application, took and examination and became an official Blue and Gold Officer for the United States Naval Academy Office of Admissions.

Finally, a chance to give back to my country! There are about 10 Blue and Gold Officers in the Las Vegas area, and each is assigned one or more high schools. The BGO works with students from those particular schools. They also conduct seminars and attend college fairs. The process is a very rewarding one.

Part of the process of applying to one of the Military Service Academies includes getting a recommendation from a U.S. Congressperson. When my friend and former colleague from UNLV, Dina Titus, was elected to serve in the U.S. House of Representatives, she asked if I would serve on her selection committee for military academy recommendations and I accepted. The committee meets only once a year in the fall. Several committee members do a group interview with each applicant. They then rate each applicant and forward the results to the Representative who in turn selects the number for which s/he has slots. U.S. Senators follow the same procedure. About one of ten applicants is admitted to each Academy

THE ACCIDENTAL USHER

After I left Nova Southeastern University, and consulting dried up as the economy turned sour, and the Blue and Gold Officer stint expired, I found myself doing little more than answering emails, sending out jokes, and writing five blogs, all with different pseudonyms. Patti prodded me to get out of the house. I was gaining weight and becoming less fit as I sat before the computer screen for hours each day.

Patti was looking for something to do as well. She had retired after 32 years as a Reading Specialist. One day she read that The Smith Center for the Performing Arts was being built next door to the Cleveland Clinic Lou Ruvo Center for Brain Health. She had begun to volunteer at the Center for Brain Health, and went to The Smith Center to see what might be available. She came home very excited and said; "We have to apply as ushers at the new theater for performing arts that is under construction. They plan to open in March and are looking for volunteers. We can work together and car pool. It will be lots of fun." Patti of course had no intention of being an usher. She knew that the theater had always been my first love. We attended regularly at the many little theaters in Las Vegas, as well as the Judy Baily Theater and Ham Hall on the UNLV campus. We used to go to London for a week and sometimes take in two shows a day. We'd gone to the theater in Los Angeles and on Broadway. Had I not gotten a formal education I'm certain I would probably have pursued a career in the performing arts.

We applied as volunteer ushers, as did Patti's close friend Teresa Moy, and we all went to the first training session together. I was immediately on cloud nine! The theater had just come alive for me. No matter that the job was "just as an usher," I could smell the greasepaint!

After the training, while driving home, Patti said, "I don't think I want to be an usher. It requires too much standing."

Teresa, "I agree. That is not my cup of tea either."

Not realizing I had just been tricked like Tom Sawyer had done to have his fence painted, I said. "Are you kidding??? This is PERFECT!" And so it was that I began a new career that has become perhaps the most satisfying of all. I am now a cog in the wheel of the part of the theater that is called, "Front of House." I am certain I will be there until they take me out feet first. No more accidents for me, even if performers do say, "Break a leg" before each performance.

SUMMARY—2013

Sometimes we get so caught up in examining the trees we overlook the forest. I was so interested in day-to-day survival from my earliest years that I rarely stepped back to see how each experience was linked and would change me from an undersized, slowly developing, shy kid who hated school, to an adult for whom school had provided hundreds of opportunities. I've had the good fortune to accidently stumble from challenge to challenge and for the most part have ended with more on the credit side of the ledger than on the debit. Even my missteps were not fatal, and they usually served as tuition for lessons in life.

I've been fortunate to have a wife who supported me when I doubted myself. I've had family and extended family that offered plenty of love.

I've also been fortunate to enjoy a modicum of success and list of accomplishments that include paperboy, box boy, entrepreneur, librarian, driver, floral deliverer, car salesman, teacher and administrator of elementary, junior high, senior high, undergraduate and graduate education, business owner, newspaper columnist, grant writer, and probably a few that I have overlooked. But perhaps the most satisfying of all my work endeavors came in "retirement." That first day that my high school English and Drama teacher, Elizabeth T. Bayless sent me onstage with a few lines to utter at the appropriate time became a defining moment in my life. From that moment onward my first love has been the theater. I put a career in the theater on hold by attending college in hopes of finding find a "real" career, and for the longest time my only association with the theater has been sitting in a cushioned seat. Except for a small role in Shakespeare's "Twelfth Night" at the UNLV Judy Bailey Theater, the theater has not been a large part of my adult life – until now. All the accidents in my life have bumped me toward my current roles in the theater; usher, merchandiser, wardrobe facilitator, and substitute supervisor at The Smith Center for the Performing Arts.

My Fifty Shades of Grades and my Journey through Wacademia were no less an adventure than Dorothy had while following the yellow brick road in the Wizard of Oz. Bravo!

(Curtain closes)

Acknowledgements

This book would not have been possible had not so many people given me a boost along the way. My father, who would not take no for an answer, and played within the system to get me into college; Mrs. Elizabeth T. Bayless who built a shred of confidence in a young shy teen with little self-confidence by putting me on stage; Mrs. Jean McKay, the Kiwi English professor who encouraged my writing; Grace Allphin, who kept my tummy full and my spirits up; Gerald "Ozzie" Nelson and Dick Priest, the best possible principals, who taught me about the principles of friendship and leadership; and so many others along the way who were quick with praise and support.

Special thanks go to my friend and professional writer Joannie Jordan who painstakingly helped edit the manuscript, offered helpful suggestions, and provided excellent direction.

Thanks to my wonderful team of Deborah Dorchak and Wendi Kelly for the cover design, formatting, providing crucial feedback, and for guiding me through the landmines that could have derailed this project.

CPSIA information can be obtained
at www.ICGtesting.com
Printed in the USA
FFHW02n1320190818
47808421-51500FF

9 780989 085403